WRAP® AND PEER SUPPORT HANDBOOK

Working Together to Reclaim Our Lives

AF854233

Mary Ellen Copeland PhD

Peach Press
Dummerston, Vermont

Email: info@WRAPandRecoveryBooks.com

WRAP and Recovery Books
PO Box 301
West Dummerston, VT 05357

WRAPandRecoveryBooks.com

Published by Peach Press, Dummerston, Vermont

Cover Design and Book Layout by Gamine Graphics.

ISBN: 978-0-9896517-6-9
Printed in the United States of America

Dedication

To my dear mother: Kate

I bet there was a lot of Peer Support going on before I first heard of it being done, being done by my mother, who had been a patient at a state asylum for eight long years, when she started gathering patients and encouraging them to talk to each other, a strategy that got her discharged so she could move on to a rich and happy life.

And to my Friend and Peer Supporter Shery Mead,

who assisted and supported me in writing this book and who has been informing my thinking about Peer Support for over 20 years.

Ever since I began studying how people who have mental health issues get well and stay well, learning from people with lived experience, I have been searching for ways to stop the human rights violations that are rampant throughout the mental health system worldwide. It has been a frustrating and daunting task. I have come to believe that the best way each one of us can protect ourselves from this inhumanity is to keep ourselves out of the system. And I believe that our best option for doing that is to consciously use WRAP and Peer Support every day.

Mary Ellen Copeland PhD

Contents

Introduction

This book is a compilation of information on WRAP and on Peer Support. It describes how these two strategies, which many people think are the gold standard for recovery, wellness and well-being, can be enhanced by using them together. It is my hope that this book will be useful to anyone: to a person who has never heard of either of these strategies, to people who know about and have used either or both of these strategies, for people who facilitate WRAP Groups and for people who arrange and implement mental health and whole health training, programs, seminars, workshops and groups.

The information in this book has been gathered from peers, compiled and tested for a long time. This process will continue into the future. It will feed the development of more and more resources on using these strategies together. Your ongoing input to info@WRAPandRecoveryBooks.com and to info@CopelandCenter.com will guide the development of these materials.

I suggest you review the book from cover to cover first, skipping over those parts that are already familiar. Then go back and read more intensively, doing some of the activities and having conversations about the discussion topics with peers. Then practice, practice, practice, referring back to this handbook as you need to. Notice positive changes in your life as a result of the work you are doing.

Section 1

Fundamentals of WRAP and Peer Support

Chapter 1

WRAP and Peer Support: How It All Began

This book is for anyone, *anyone at all*, who wants to use WRAP and Peer Support, including people with all kinds of mental and physical health challenges, peers, health care providers, family members and friends. It is also for anyone who has experienced the effects of trauma in their lives, people who want to get past the effects of this trauma, to do the things they want to do and be the way they want to be.

WRAP Group Facilitators, people who work with others to develop WRAP, and people who want to enhance their understanding of WRAP and Peer Support will find that this book is a valuable guide.

Wrap Group Facilitators will enhance their facilitation skills in ways that support building and sustaining relationships while working on the development of WRAP. WRAP is often used as an individual tool to enhance lives and promote well being. Using WRAP with Peer Support may generate conversations and lead to solutions that would not be considered when working alone. Given the group model that has evolved for developing WRAP, incorporating a Peer Support component is appropriate to its values, and has the potential for expanding possibilities that had not been previously considered.

WRAP and Peer Support were developed, not in the conference rooms of famous universities by learned scholars, but by the people who needed them the most, people who had experienced challenges in their own day-to-day lives.

Even now, people who are surviving trauma are receiving punitive treatment and are living out their lives locked in institutions where they have little opportunity to move forward in their lives. And too many people are choosing to end their lives because they see no way out of the horrific pain they live with every day, every moment. I believe that Peer Support, and WRAP with Peer Support, are solutions to these pressing issues.

> *By putting into practice WRAP and Peer Support, people can work together to move beyond the challenges in their lives on their own and with the support of others. With planning and practice, people can effectively avoid the human rights violations, abuse and trauma, restraint, seclusion, electroshock therapy, use of psychiatric medications, humiliation and short or long term incarceration, that have been the cornerstone of so-called mental health treatment, as far back as we know.*

Even people who are already deeply entrenched in the system can use what they learn in WRAP and Peer Support to begin and continue the process of making their lives the way they want them to be. People who have been in institutions for months or years, or whose lives are compromised, will find a place to begin their way back.

The Development of WRAP with Peer Support

When I think about where WRAP came from, my thoughts go back in time, much further than I thought they would go. They go back to when I was a very little girl, eight years old, lonely and frightened, as a nurse with lots of keys unlocked numerous heavy doors, leading me and my siblings to the large, noisy and scary room where we would have our weekly visit with our mother. She had been taken to that institution after she experienced deep and seemingly intractable depression, and after my father had been told that she was incurably insane.

Our visits were brief and impersonal. It was hard to find the woman we remembered as "Ma" in the midst of multitudes of agitated people, pacing, crying, screaming and often interrupting any semblance of a conversation we were trying to have with our mother, who was walking in circles and repeating over and over words we couldn't understand. I think WRAP began there, in the mind of a small girl who became convinced that what was happening here was wrong and bad, that there was no chance anyone could get well and stay well in this circumstance, where the only treatments were an occasional ceramics class and barbaric electroshock treatments. (They were really barbaric in the old days, irrespective of how they are viewed today.)

In spite of all, after eight years in that horrible place, my mother did get well. How did she do that? Peer Support. She had never talked much to anyone about anything personal. But then a volunteer at the hospital started asking her questions and she began to talk—and she talked and she talked and she talked. She kept apologizing to the volunteer who kept encouraging and supporting her, validating her experiences and asking her more questions. They became fast friends—and peers. One of the nurses started to do the same thing. She was also a peer. My mother had never, never talked so much. And as she talked she felt better and better and better. So she did something outlandish. My mother was outlandish to begin with, so this was not out of character. She started gathering other patients together in small groups and encouraged and supported them in talking to each other, in sharing the horror that made up their lives, and figuring out ways to move forward. That didn't go over very well at the hospital, so they discharged her.

She came home and gradually, over time, picked up the pieces of her life and moved on. But she kept connection with her peers that she had left behind, even going back for meetings of the groups she had started. I don't think I would have had the courage to do that. And she built for herself, over time, a circle of mutual support that sustained her as she made her way back into the world.

I think at that point, the possibility that people might recover became a little clearer for me. I watched what was happening, and as I look back, wish I had been more supportive, rather than a typical somewhat difficult teenager, away at college and building a life of my own. I saw how she built those new, supportive relationships, pursued her long dormant career as a dietician and worked to maintain her wellness and continue her recovery with a lot of support from peers, too little support from family and none from care providers. What a brave woman!

Through this time I went to college, got married, had a family, and was diverted from that niggling thought in my mind, "People can get over this." But I was a self-help "junkie." I read every self-help book and article I could get my hands on. And, because I was experiencing deep depressions in my own life, I tried the things I learned. And a lot of them helped—especially relaxation and stress reduction techniques, diet, exercise and building strong mutual relationships.

I raised my children, began a career, and life moved along in spite of the depressions and some expansive moods that were becoming almost a constant companion. And still the thought lingered in the back of my mind. "There is something you can do. People don't need to go through this." I took that thought out, dusted it off and reviewed it from time to time, and then it settled back into its place at the back of my mind.

And then something happened that catapulted that thought into clear view. I had been overworking and leading a stressful life. I was in a bad marriage and had many more responsibilities than any one person should have. In the process of getting out of the marriage and trying to rebuild my life, my times of deep sadness increased, and also some puzzling times when for no good reason I felt absolutely terrific, better than I had ever felt in my life. At times my moods were so expansive that I thought I could do anything at all, even fly, and I enjoyed them so much that I failed to notice the ominous signs that were becoming so clear to family members and friends.

After finding myself with no work or means to support myself, and after repeated hospitalizations (the best thing about them was the Peer Support—I am still closely connected to one of the peers that I met in an early hospitalization) and trials on stronger and stronger medications, I said to my psychiatrist, "How do people like me recover? How do they get well, stay well and get on with their lives?" He said he would get that information for me for the next appointment.

I looked forward to the next appointment with great anticipation. Finally I was going to get some information that would lead me out of this morass. Imagine my disappointment when he told me that there was no information of that kind. He said, "We have information on medication options and on treatment programs, but nothing on how people get well and move on with their lives." I was astounded. And it was then that the thought that had been dormant in my mind for so long decided to stir. It said, "You need to talk to people like yourself—people who have all these horrid 'symptoms' and life experiences. You need to ask them what helps. If you get information from enough people, you will be able to figure out what to do for yourself."

I devised a plan that I would develop a survey and ask people like me to fill it out. I didn't really know the questions to ask so I made them open-ended, hoping if people wrote a lot, I could glean some answers, and then perhaps even figure out some new questions from what they had told me. I thought I could get volunteers by putting short articles in various mental health newsletters.

I told my vocational rehabilitation counselor about this grandiose scheme, fully expecting a rebuff. After all, I had been living with out of control "mood swings" for quite a long time. "Why should anyone have any confidence in me?" To my surprise she said, "What a great idea!" Then she proceeded to help me develop a Social Security Plan to Achieve Self Sufficiency that would give me money for a computer, paper and supplies for the surveys, postage and phone—enough to get me started.

It was slow going at first. I was trying to cope with deep depression, lack of motivation, low self-confidence, anxiety, lethargy and general malaise. But somewhere inside of me there was a spark that kept me going as I set up a working space for myself in my tiny apartment, learned how to use a computer and developed articles to put in mental health publications to find peers who would volunteer. I wasn't ready for the positive response I received. I got hundreds of phone calls and letters (this was before email). I ended up with 125 people who said they were willing to respond to a series of questions that might give me some insights on how people with various kinds of mental health difficulties cope on a daily basis, how they work toward meeting their life goals and what helps them to feel better when they are not feeling well.

My next project was to develop the surveys. I decided I would have three surveys. People could send me back the first one and I could use what I learned to develop the second one and then, in the same way the third, building each time on what I had discovered through the last surveys. People who do research gave me a really hard time. They said it would never work. Some even made fun of what they said were my primitive attempts at research. They said I would never be able to compile the data from the open-ended questions I was using. They said I should ask a question and then rate the answer, 5, 4, 3, 2, 1, a process I had no interest in at all. I did not even know at this point what questions to ask. I had to develop some questions that were my best guess at what might get people sharing, and then use this sharing to develop questions that were more targeted toward getting useful information.

I got the most information from a blank space that I left at the end of each section and at the back of the survey. It was amazing. People, my peers, were so anxious to share. They said no one had ever asked them for this kind of information. They wrote up the sides and all over the front and back of the survey booklets. Some sent in tape recordings and articles from magazines.

As these survey booklets began piling up in my living room the task that lay ahead seemed insurmountable. How was I to compile this information in a way that made sense or could be helpful to anyone? Gradually I developed a system that seemed to work. And as I input data, I began to see patterns emerge. Things my peers did to help themselves became clearer and clearer. I learned about support groups, Crisis Plans, maintaining key relationships, diet, light, exercise and numerous "tricks" that help you feel better. I learned how people managed their medications and their relationships with health care providers. I learned how people made the best of hospital stays and how they avoided them.

The more information I compiled from these amazing people, the more changes I made in my own life. And I started feeling better and better. Now with new energy and enthusiasm, I set up a couple of workshops to share my findings. A health care provider told me I could never give a workshop—but I did. It was packed and people loved it. They shared more and more and more. And I learned more and more and more.

The word got out and I was asked to present on my findings at a national "mental illness" conference, my first trip since my mental health had become so troublesome. They gave me a small room to present in, thinking my subject matter would be of little interest. I was a "client" after all, and had to wear a green ribbon to let everyone know that. The room was jam-packed and people were standing in the hall trying to get in. It was a huge success.

That was a beginning for me. People started asking me to come to their area and lead workshops. To do that, I began to compile the information into a book so I would have something to hand out to participants. The book was so popular that I sent it off to several publishers for possible publication. Some people shook their heads and told me the publishers wouldn't even look at it. But before long a publisher called me and said they wanted to publish the book. I was off and running.

For the next few years I traveled, taught about what I had learned, wrote several more books and had them published, all while continuing to work on my wellness and rebuild my life. I worked myself off of Social Security and even bought a home of my own.

Then in 1997, something remarkable happened. I was working with a group of peers, people who were using mental health services in northern Vermont, along with some care providers and family members. On the last day of our eight all-day sessions together, a woman stood up and said, "This is all well and good, but I have been in state hospitals across the country and I wouldn't have any idea how to organize these tools and strategies in my life."

In response, Jane Winterling and I facilitated this group of peers as they developed (and so aptly named), the Wellness Recovery Action Plan, now well known as WRAP. It sounded great to me, so I went home and developed one for myself. And it moved me to a new level of wellbeing. I thought it was so good that I decided to share it at a conference where I was leading a workshop. There I was greeted by a group of people, obviously worn from studying chemical drug formulas and looking at brain slides. I apprehensively presented WRAP. They loved it. The response was overwhelmingly positive.

After that, whenever I led a workshop or spoke at conference, people just wanted to know about WRAP. That summer I wrote the popular red WRAP book which has now sold many thousands of copies. In addition I developed a curriculum to teach people how to lead WRAP Groups and began holding several WRAP Facilitator seminars each year.

Since then WRAP has grown enormously. It got so big that we had to develop the not-for-profit Copeland Center for Wellness and Recovery just to handle the numerous requests for WRAP trainings all over the world. I continue to develop WRAP related resources. They include resources like A WRAP Workbook for Kids, WRAP for Veterans and People in the Military, Spanish WRAP, WRAP for Addictions, WRAP for Life, WRAP Plus, Living WRAP DVD, and other DVDs and CDs. These resources are available from WRAPandRecoveryBooks.com.

The exciting thing about this work is the stories I hear from peers about how WRAP, and the Values and Ethics that have evolved from it, have affected, transformed and even saved people's lives, how it has done the same thing for people who teach others about WRAP, and even for the mental health system as a whole.

WRAP has been a Peer Support initiative from its beginning. The focus of this book will be on how to effectively use the two together—WRAP and Peer Support. To get the information for this book, I have collaborated with Shery Mead, who developed Intentional Peer Support, with Gina Calhoun and Matthew Federici of the Copeland Center for Wellness and Recovery, and with people everywhere who have responded to my queries. In addition, I have reached out to people who use WRAP, WRAP Group Facilitators, Advanced Level WRAP Facilitators and to people who understand the value of Peer Support.

Chapter 2

Overview of the Wellness Recovery Action Plan

This Chapter is a basic overview of the Wellness Recovery Action Plan. Chapters 3, 4 and 5 describe Peer Support in more detail. Chapter 6 describes the common Values and Ethics of WRAP and Peer Support, Chapter 7 describes why WRAP and Peer Support work together and Chapter 8 has Guidelines for Using WRAP and Peer Support Together. The second section of the book will walk you step-by-step through the process of developing and using WRAP with Peer Support.

The Wellness Recovery Action Plan is a straightforward life and wellness planning process that people can develop for themselves if and when they want to. It includes developing lists of resources (the Wellness Toolbox) and then using those resources to develop Action Plans, including a Daily Maintenance Plan, identifying Triggers, Early Warning Signs and signs that Things are Getting Much Worse or Breaking Down (also known as Avoiding a Crisis) and Action Plans for each, then a Crisis Plan or Advance Directive and a Post Crisis Plan.

WRAP is recognized as an evidence-based program and practice by the National Registry of Evidence Based Programs and Practices (NREPP) (United States) http://www.nrepp.samhsa.gov/ViewIntervention.aspx?id=208 because it has been intensively studied in rigorous and extensive research projects and proven to be effective (www.mentalhealthrecovery.com). WRAP is a planning process that involves assessing the self-help tools and resources that we have or that we might want to try, and then using those tools and resources to develop plans for living well, whatever that means to us, and for navigating difficult times.

The Wellness Recovery Action Plan, as described here, is just as it was devised in 1997 by a group of people who had been mental health service users for many years, with the addition of a Post Crisis Plan that was suggested by someone who was enmeshed in the system who felt a Post Crisis Plan was needed to close the circle between that time when you were moving out of a very difficult time (crisis) and are back to once again using the Daily Maintenance section of WRAP.

Wellness Toolbox

The first part of WRAP is developing a personal Wellness Toolbox. This is a list of resources used to develop WRAP. It includes things like contacting friends and supporters, peer counseling, focusing exercises, relaxation and stress reduction exercises, journaling, creative, fun and affirming activities like writing poetry, painting or woodcraft, exercise, diet, light, and sleep. It can be a long or a short list. Many people find that at first their list is short, but over time, as they have more experience, they discover many more Wellness Tools. I used to have just a few things on my list. Now I have over 80. I have come to realize that even things like petting my dog, taking a break, or even working, can be Wellness Tools, depending on when and how I use them.

Daily Maintenance Plan

Section 1 of WRAP is the **Daily Maintenance Plan**. It includes three parts:

1. A description of yourself when, by your own assessment, you feel quite good. This is a reminder for those times when you have not been feeling the way you want to feel for some time and forget what that feels like. It also keeps you in touch with what you want to feel like, what you are working toward. Most people write a list of descriptive words, like introverted, out-going, competent, responsible, flamboyant, introspective or content. It could be several paragraphs or a poem. It could include a picture or anything else the person feels gives an accurate picture of who they are, by their own assessment, in the best of times.

2. Those Wellness Tools you know you must use every day to keep yourself feeling the way you want to feel and being the way you want to be. This was a wake-up call for me. I became aware that if I used certain Wellness Tools every day I felt quite happy and healthy most of the time. This list should be short so that it can be easily accomplished each day along with all of the other things we do to make our lives rich and rewarding. When I was speaking to a group, a man who was enmeshed in the mental health system said, "If only I had known 20 years ago that there are things I can do to help myself, my life would have been very different."

3. Part three of the Daily Maintenance section is a list of things a person might need to do on any given day. It's a daily assessment of what might need to be done, like a making a doctor's appointment, contacting a family member, buying groceries, paying bills or getting a haircut. You can add in things you need to do weekly, monthly or even every year, if you want to.

Listing things I need to do every day was very important to me. I came to realize that if I was sure to do certain things each day, I really felt quite good. And if I got "off track" and didn't do some things in my plan, I noticed the difference right away.

Triggers

Section 2 is identifying those events that, if they happened, might make you feel worse. They might be unexpected or they might be things you can anticipate, things like an argument with a friend, getting a big bill, the loss of a pet, being treated badly, being reminded of something difficult that happened in your past or the anniversary of loss. Even good things like birthdays or winning a prize can be upsetting. The people who developed WRAP wanted them to be called Triggers. Then, using Wellness Tools, you develop an Action Plan you can use to get through this difficult time. This list can include many options, because you never know when in your life you might be face-to-face with something upsetting. The possibilities of what you might do at that time would vary depending on the circumstances. One of the Wellness Tools I use most often at times like this, if something unexpected that is difficult happens, is to have a dialogue with a peer. And sometimes, depending on the circumstances, I find a quiet space and spend a few minutes contemplating the situation and deciding how to respond.

Early Warning Signs

Section 3 is identifying **Early Warning Signs**, those subtle signs that let people know that they are beginning to feel worse, like being unable to sleep, or feelings of nervousness. Before WRAP, and before developing awareness that I could do things for myself that would help me feel better, I ignored these signs and usually ended up feeling worse and worse and worse. Signs that I began to notice were that I stop buckling my seat belt, was careless about watching for traffic when I cross the street, a hard knot in my chest, aches and pains, and waking up at 3 in the morning and not being able to get back to sleep.

Then, again using the Wellness Toolbox, developing an Action Plan for responding to these signs so that you feel better quickly and prevent a possible more difficult time. When I notice Early Warning Signs, I take a two-hour break and do one of my favorite things, like going for a long walk or doing some kind of art or quilting. If I don't feel better after that, I take the whole next day off to do fun things on my Wellness Tool list. I have found that I have many choices—choices that I had ignored in the past—pre-WRAP.

When Things Are Breaking Down (Avoiding a Crisis)

Section 4 is **When Things Are Breaking Down (Avoiding a Crisis)**. In this section, you list those signs that are, for you, indicators that you are feeling much worse, things like feeling very sad all the time, not being able to hold your head up and look at others, crying continually for hours, not sleeping at all for two nights, acute, persistent pain, or persistently hearing troubling voices. These are only examples. Each of us knows what the signs are for us, or we can figure them out using Peer Support. Then, using your Wellness Tools, you develop a powerful Action Plan that will help you feel better as quickly as possible and prevent an even more difficult time. When this happens to me, I use the plans I have developed for at least three days—more if needed. These intensive and directive plans include visits to my counselor, time with peers (even by Skype if needed), good food, exercise, time outdoors and lots of time listing to music I love and doing those things I enjoy. It works for me. I have had difficult times and have been able to "back them off."

Crisis Plan or Advance Directive

Section 5 is a **Crisis Plan or Advance Directive**. In the Crisis Plan, the person who is developing the plan identifies:

- Signs that let others know they need to take over responsibility for your care and decision-making, like substance abuse, being abusive to others or certain compulsive behaviors
- Who you want to take over for you and support you through this time
- Health care information
- A plan for staying at home through this time if at all possible
- Things others can do that would help and things they might choose to do that would not be helpful

This kind of proactive advance planning keeps the person whose life it is in control even when it seems like things are out of control. People give copies of this part of the plan to all those people they listed as supporters so they know just what to do.

What I have seen happen is that, with WRAP, what people have identified as a crisis has changed dramatically. I used to consider it a crisis if I was crying and unable to stop crying, if I was thinking a lot about ending my life and even telling others that I was feeling that way, that I was abusing substances, and that I was taking risks that were clearly dangerous. Now those same things are signs for me that "Things are Breaking Down" and I know what to do move myself out of that place. So, for me now, my Crisis Plan is for when I am unconscious or unresponsive. This is a big change.

In working on this book, I got another vision of what a crisis might be for some people. I thought about my mother who was in a horrific institution for eight years. (You can read Kate's story at mentalhealthrecovery.com.)

I thought of other people like her, who are stuck, for short or long periods of time, in institutions or untenable situations. This would include various kinds of care homes, prisons, jails, and mental institutions. We can use the Crisis Plan and then the Post Crisis Plan to work ourselves, small step by small step, out of these horrid situations and back into life—using Peer Support to help us figure out the path

Post Crisis Plan

Section 6 is the **Post Crisis Plan**. This part of the plan deals with that difficult time right after you have had a crisis, when you are trying to heal and get back to feeling good again. It is a list of questions. Most people just review this part and know that it is there if they ever need it. You may want to think about this part of the plan in advance and even write some things to do in that time. However, you may want to write most of it as you are beginning to recover from the crisis—when you have a clearer picture of what you need to do for yourself to get well. As with the Crisis Plan, this part of the plan can be used to get yourself out of, or get by the best you can, when you find yourself in horrific situations where you feel like you have lost all control.

Using WRAP

Before I had a WRAP, I was convinced that I was "manic depressive" (now called bipolar disorder), that I could never get well, that I had no control over what was happening to me and that I often had no control over my behavior. I was even told that I would likely get worse over time.

As I learned more and more about mental health recovery from people who had some of the same experiences I did, I began to question my label, my diagnosis. I was beginning to understand that some of the terrible things that had happened to me in my life were causing deep depression, and out-of-control behavior. I began to see that I had choices, that I could have control over what was happening to me and my life, I could definitely change my behavior and that I could respond to difficult times in different ways, even when I had sad feelings, suicidal thoughts and severe anxiety.

Using WRAP, I do things every day (or at least most days) to keep myself feeling the way I want to feel. If I begin to feel sad, anxious or upset, I have learned that I can live with those uncomfortable feelings without being in any danger. I can use simple Wellness Tools to help myself move forward—things like getting together with a peer and talking about what I am experiencing (my most important Wellness Tool), reading a good book, making some music, taking a walk or doing some deep breathing or yoga. I might cook myself a healthy meal or ask my partner to do it with me.

People use their WRAP every day, noting how they feel and doing what they need to do to get better and well, or do the best they can to cope with the situation they find themselves in. As people become familiar with their plan, they find that the review process takes less time and that they know how to respond without even referring to their plan. People who are using these plans regularly and updating them as necessary, are finding that they have fewer difficult times, and that when they do have a hard time it is not as bad as it used to be and it doesn't last as long.

WRAP empowers people to take control of their own health and wellness. Since its development, it has been shared with millions of people all over the world through WRAP Groups, training, seminars, and the many WRAP resources I have developed in consultation with WRAP users world-wide.

WRAPandRecoveryBooks.com and the Copeland Center for Wellness and Recovery at CopelandCenter.com are the authorized sources for WRAP resources and training.

Most people learn about WRAP in small informal groups sponsored by mental health agencies or organizations. This seems to work best as people in these groups learn so much from each other. These groups are usually led by WRAP Facilitators who are trained by the Copeland Center for Wellness and Recovery. But many, many people develop WRAP on their own using one or several of the WRAP resources, or with a supportive peer, care provider, friend or family member. There are now WRAP programs in all kinds of institutions. If you are in an institution and there is no WRAP program, you can develop your WRAP on your own, or even better, with a peer using Peer Support as described in this book.

If you are in an institution or a situation where you don't have access to any WRAP resources or even a notebook to write in, you can start "thinking WRAP" as a way to begin your journey toward whatever it is you want. You can think about things, even little things you can do to walk yourself out of the situation you are in that is unacceptable to you. If you can talk it through with someone else, it will support you in remembering and putting your thoughts into action. If you find yourself thinking that there is no one to talk to about this, no one to engage in a dialogue, think about talking to other people whose situation is similar to yours, using the techniques and strategies described in this book. Anyone, anywhere can develop a WRAP, even if it is just in your mind.

In traditional mental health programs, others often developed our treatment and life plans—sometimes without even consulting us. I remember being shown my "Treatment Plan." At the top was a list of goals. But they were not my goals. Someone else had decided what my goals should be. The activities that they described that I was to use to meet these goals were of no interest to me. I even found some of them to be distasteful. Others were trying to take over control of every aspect of my life, including where I would live, who my friends would be, what I would do for work, what I would do with my leisure time, how my "symptoms" would be treated, and what would happen to me if they got worse. This made me feel disempowered and worse than ever.

WRAP is the opposite of that. WRAP is totally voluntary. You, and only you, decide if and when you want to develop a WRAP. Everything in your WRAP comes directly from you. You decide which parts you do and which you leave out. It is based on the premise that you are the expert on yourself and that you are the best one to figure out what will and what won't work for you. You also decide who you want to support you in developing your WRAP, who you share it with and who you don't share it with.

WRAP is a self-designed plan for staying well, and for helping you to feel better when you are not feeling well, to increase personal responsibility and control over your own life, and help you make your life the way you want it to be.

Chapter 3

Peer Support

As more and more peers have Peer Support skills, we increase our ability to reflect on all the relationships in our lives and what makes them work. In doing this we're working towards personal and social change. That is the role of Peer Support, and it is a very important one. Shery Mead

Before combining WRAP and Peer Support, you need to know what Peer Support is. The broad definition of Peer Support, as it is used in the mental health system, is when two or more people with similar experiences get together in person or electronically to share their experiences, to learn together how to move past the difficulties this has created in their lives, to give each other hope, and to support each other as they do the things they want to do and make their lives the way they want them to be. Peer Support can be used by anyone with any kind of life experience.

Peer Support is not as easy to understand and implement as WRAP because there is no set process and there are many, many options. The next chapter, Peer Support Methods and Strategies, will describe many of those options, but how you implement it will be your choice.

Peer Support is not the same as friends, family members or colleagues getting together for an informal chat.

Before using Peer Support when developing a Wellness Recovery Action Plan, read, reread and discuss with your peers Section 1 of this book. This work deserves this close attention. If some things are hard to understand, do role-plays with peers and discuss the issues with peers until what you are doing feels right to both or all of you.

In Peer Support, the participants are the experts.

Peer Support enhances the process of developing a Wellness Recovery Action Plan by giving people the opportunity to discuss things they are considering, by learning of other people's experiences and by sharing and exploring options. Many formats have been used successfully, whether it is two people working together, a WRAP Group that meets once or several times a week, or even in a larger WRAP workshop or seminar that meets for a full day, several days in a week.

Many of us who have spent time in the mental health system have learned how to be "patients" instead of people. After you've been given a "mental illness" diagnosis and begun to use services designed for people with "mental illness," you may feel like you are inferior to other people, and begin to think about all aspects of your life as if you were a "mental patient." You may become, in your own mind and the mind of others, a diagnosis rather than a person. You may feel separated from others and de-valued.

The hope is that, using Peer Support, you can move past these old views of yourself, and begin seeing yourself as the same as everyone else. This supports you as you move forward in your life, as you recover and do the things you want to do and be the way you want to be. You do this by practicing relationships in Peer Support in ways that may be less familiar to you, but that help you to remember who you really are and what you are working toward.

> *Instead of taking care of each other and thinking of each other as "mentally ill," in Peer Support we build a sense of community where we are responsible to each other, and where we focus on learning together, moving forward in our lives, on recovery and wellness, and on working toward our dreams and goals.*
>
> *Peer Support is different from the support you get from counselors, doctors and case managers. It is more than just being friends. In Peer Support you understand each other because, although everyone has their own unique stories, you have similar experiences that can create a bond that allows you to learn together, to figure out how to change the way you do things and the way you think, and to figure out how to move forward in your lives, building relationships that are respectful of each other, where you are responsible to each other, and that support you in creating the change you want in your lives. By sharing your experiences and building trust in each other, you learn to go forward in new ways that move you away from seeing yourself as "mentally ill" and the limitations of such a view. In Peer Support, you can safely try out new ideas and new ways of being through "learning" rather than a "treatment."*

Peer Support is often not easy. You may have been strongly influenced by the mental health and other systems (health care, education, marriage, etc.) that have developed in our society. It can be hard to change those ways of doing things and the beliefs and assumptions that supported them. Sometimes in Peer Support, because of old habits, you do the things to others that were done to you. You may try to "help" each other by suggesting more medication, by getting together behind closed doors and "figuring out" what to do with a "difficult" person, or by teasing, bullying or trying to control others. Using Peer Support, you can figure out responses that move you forward rather that keep you stuck in old ways of being that didn't work for you.

What Peer Support Isn't

Peer Support is not counseling or therapy. It is not analyzing another person.

Peer Support is not judging another person or other people.

Peer Support is not giving advice or telling a person or other people what they should do or what they must do.

Peer Support does not make assumptions about another person or other people.

Peer Support is not about taking care of the other person or people.

While your first contact with someone in the mental health system may have been around "mental illness" or mental health issues or difficulties, in Peer Support, the first conversation is usually about experiences. It is sharing in ways that support creating change in the way people see themselves and in creating the change they want in their lives. One person might say to another, "Tell me about the most recent experience you've had doing something you didn't think you could do?" That would lead to a different conversation than "What kind of medication are you using to treat your depression?"

One day when I went to a meeting at the local community mental health center, I was really affected by what I saw. There on the smoking porch were many of the members of our peer program. They were waiting to get their medications and their social security check. People kept their heads down, shuffled around and looked rather defeated. What limited conversation they did have focused almost exclusively on illness. People talked about their various crises, need for appointments, why they needed more money from their payee, etc. Maybe you're thinking that this would not be an unusual conversation for a mental health center and it probably isn't.

The interesting thing was that these very same people had a completely different kind of conversation at the peer center. It was always energetic and lively. People talked about their friends and their weekends. They talked about politics and what should happen at the peer center. It was like night and day. This led me to believe that not only do we have our own cultural experience, but that we shape how we behave to fit the way we think others perceive us and to the environment we're in. Shery Mead

In conversations, you may talk about yourself based on what you think the listener assumes about you. If you've spent a lot of time in the mental health system, you may have learned to tell people your "mental illness story" (your diagnosis, when it began, the medications you are taking, medication side effects, hospitalizations, day treatment programs and being on disability). In Peer Support you focus on the real story of who you are, where you have been, what's happened to you and how you want to move forward. You learn to tell your story based on who's listening, how much you trust them, what impact you want to have, your assumptions about the way they think and how the conversation can move both of you forward in some way.

Discussion Topics

Is this description of Peer Support the same as, or different from, what you thought Peer Support was? If so, describe what you thought it was. Which do you think would work better for you and why?

Describe times when you have used Peer Support. How did they work for you? Did they give you hope? Did you learn together? Did you both move forward?

Do you think Peer Support would work well for you? Why or why not?

Who can be Peer Supporters?

A Peer Supporter can be anyone who shares common experiences with the other person or people. Any two people could find some common experience, so that means anybody could be a Peer Supporter if they are willing to follow the agreed upon Values and Ethics of Peer Support and work with the methods and strategies that have been found to work over time.

In mental health, Peer Support generally refers to people working together who have experience as users of the mental health system. But it doesn't have to be limited to that circumstance. For example, one person may have used mental health services and be a peer with another person because of age-related issues or sexual orientation issues.

Because Peer Support is recognized as a valuable recovery tool, mental health agencies and organizations are hiring people who have used the mental health system as "Peer Support Specialists". This provides income for people with valued expertise, who might otherwise be unemployed or employed in positions that don't match their interests or skills. However, when one person is getting paid and the other is not, it creates a "difference" that may have to be addressed. People who are Peer Supporters can address these issues as they work and learn together.

Attributes of Peer Supporters

How can you know if you could be a Peer Supporter? In making this decision, be honest with yourself. It is not fair to others if you are not the right person to be a Peer Supporter, or the Peer Supporter for a person who is difficult for you to be with and to interact with. It is not a negative reflection on you if you can't be a Peer Supporter or you can't be a Peer Supporter for certain people. This is not something that everyone would want to do, would like to do, or would feel comfortable doing.

In considering if you are the right person to be a Peer Supporter, consider the following questions. Before you make a final decision, you may want to read the rest of this chapter and even the rest of this book. Then you will know if Peer Support is something you want to do and can do.

1. Are you flexible in your thinking? Do you like to discuss your views and other people's views? (Or do you have certain set ideas and standards that you are not willing to consider or change that might make Peer Support difficult for you?)
2. Can you accept and be respectful of all kinds of diversity, with relation to things like age, gender, sexual orientation, economic status, ethnic background, educational status, learning ability, disability, race, life experience and religious preference?
3. Can you empathize with others who are having a difficult time, even if you don't agree with what they are doing or how they are feeling?
4. Can you accept another person's or other people's perspective as belonging to them, even if it is different from your own? (Peer Support

Chapter 4

Peer Support Concepts

This chapter describes the concepts that will guide you as you "do" Peer Support. The focus of the next chapter is the Peer Support process.

Learning Together

In Peer Support people *learn together*. Learning together takes time and dialogue. It is about working together to uncover new information, learn new things and learn new ways of doing things. When people learn together, whether they are working on a WRAP or on any kind of issue, it opens up options and ideas that individuals may not have thought of on their own, increasing the likelihood of an even more effective and successful outcome.

Learning together is not the same as helping one another. Many of the relationships in our lives have the goal of helping rather than learning together—like the relationships you had when you received services. Many people are used to being in a "helping" role, especially when the other person says they are having a difficult time. This can interfere with learning together, and with uncovering new and different ways of being. It can create an inequality in the relationship where one person is being helped and the other person is the helper.

Following is an example of where *helping might get in the way* of learning together:

Lester: I'd like your help to do my WRAP plan.

Molly: I'd love to help. WRAP really saved my life.

Lester: Really, I'm not so sure about it. It feels really hard to me.

Molly: It's not hard at all. In fact, once I got going on it, it was really easy. I bet if we just start talking about your Wellness Tools, you'll get into it.

Lester: I don't really have any Wellness Tools.

Molly: Well some of mine are: eating three healthy meals a day, going for a walk and meditation. Would any of those fit for you?

Lester: I guess.

In his response, "I guess," it feels like Lester is giving in to Molly's enthusiasm and her "help." Without knowing any of the reasons why Lester may have found WRAP challenging, Molly has talked Lester into trying what she thinks are good ideas for him. Even if Lester finds some of the things she says to be helpful, he may not stick with the plan, as it wasn't really his idea to begin with.

Following is the same scenario with a focus on *learning together*:

Lester: I'd really like your help with my WRAP Plan.

Molly: That sounds great. Why are you interested in a WRAP plan?

Lester: I have heard that they work well for a lot of people, but to be honest with you, I've tried doing them before and found it really challenging.

Molly: I remember finding it challenging myself when I started out. I felt quite frustrated at times.

Lester: Yeah, all these other people seem to be doing them and I just can't seem to get it.

Molly: When you said you can't get it, what do you think you can't get?

Lester: It seems like everyone else can come up with Wellness Tools so easily and I can't think of any.

Molly: You know, when I first started doing WRAP I had a hard time thinking of Wellness Tools as well.

Lester: Really?

Molly: I even adopted other people's Wellness Tools for a while so I could try something, but that didn't work very well.

Lester: So what did you do?

Molly: It's really good to be talking about it because I hadn't really realized that I'd done that until now. I guess what I did was just really paid attention to the kinds of things that made me feel better about myself and over time I figured some things out.

Lester: Yes, I guess I've always wanted a quick fix or instant gratification so I suppose I've made some half-hearted attempts at change but the things I've been successful at changing took me a while.

Through this conversation Lester and Molly learn together as equals.

Discussion Topics

What does Learning Together mean to you? Describe situations where you worked with other people to figure out new ways of thinking and new ways of doing things, where you learned together. How did you like it? How did it work for you? How does it differ from help?

Moving Forward

You will hear the words Moving Forward over and over in this book. I like the word recovery but I like the words Moving Forward even better. It seems to more accurately represent what I am working on with my WRAP—Moving Forward. Using Peer Support Concepts you learn in this chapter, the Peer Support Process you learn in the next chapter, the skills and strategies that are described in this book, and those you figure out for yourself, you and the people you are "doing" Peer Support with figure out new ways of being and doing things that have the potential to move you forward, that take you to where you want to be in your life.

When you are sharing experiences with each other in Peer Support, you use your combined experience and knowledge to "move forward," perhaps making changes in the ways you do things and the things you do that feel better and more right to you. Moving forward is what this work is all about, moving from one place in your life to another place in your life that feels better and more right to you. The changes may be small or they may be big—wherever you are in your life and whatever you feel is right to do.

Examples of Moving Forward

Tom told Marcy that he has a hard time figuring out what he needs to do every day to keep himself well, but that he is getting better at it since he heard how other people were doing it in the WRAP Group—putting lists on the refrigerator and keeping supplies on hand. Marcy says that is not always easy for her either, but over time she has gotten used to doing the things she knows she needs to do every day. She says motivation is sometimes hard for her but knows Tom has some experience with this and he shares ideas that she says she will try.

Jack and Sarah were talking about college. Jack said he always wanted to go to college but was afraid it would be too much for him. He said that seeing himself as a mental patient had made him feel fragile and incapable of taking a major step like this. Sarah said that after being hospitalized several times for deep sadness, she noticed that she started giving up plans for her life that were important to her, like going on to school and having a family. She told Jack that she had overcome those hurdles and moved on and was sure that he could too. Jack asked her more questions about making that change and noticed that he was beginning to feel more hopeful about taking the next steps so that he could go to college.

Discussion Topics

What does "moving forward" mean to you? How does it differ from words like recovery, wellness and prevention? Which of these words do you prefer? How do you use them in your life?

Describe times in your life when it was hard to feel motivated and to "move forward"? Describe how you got through that time. How do you think Peer Support might help you get through such a time?

Mutuality

Peer Support is about working together as equals while paying close attention to the relationship. This may be different from the way you are used to doing things, especially if you have been in the mental health system and have been working with people like doctors and case managers, where the relationship is not mutual. Peer Support is not about one person doing something to or for someone else. It is not for the benefit of one person. It is for the benefit of both people and, in a WRAP Group, of everyone who is involved.

In mutual relationships, people talk through differences, share feelings and support each other. Each person is fully present to the other person, listening for their story and their feelings and their meanings, even when they are unspoken.

In a mutual relationship there are no predetermined outcomes and no goals. Instead of trying to persuade the other person to do something or think a particular way, you are each trying to understand what the other person is saying, thinking about your responses, and sharing what seems most important to share.

Mutuality applies to listening, just as it applies to all Peer Support. From time to time, I have been a Peer Supporter for someone who is in a lot of distress. If this was the situation, I used to think it was best to forego my time to be heard. I gave up mutuality in deference to what I felt was the other person's need. It didn't work well for either of us. I have learned over time that mutuality pertains at all times and that both people need to share and be heard.

Following is an example of mutual support:

Sally: Hi Anna. It's good to see you! How are you?

Anna: I'm a bit better thanks. I've been thinking about what you were telling me about the WRAP plan, and I think I'd like to work on one.

Sally: Oh, that's great! When would you like to start?

Anna: Right now would be good. Where do we start?

Sally: Well, the first part is talking about what we call Wellness Tools.

Anna: OK, what are some of yours?

Sally: You know, I'm happy to share with you some of my Wellness Tools, but I think I'd prefer to spend a bit of time getting to know each other first. We each have things that we can learn from each other. If I just tell you what I did, it won't make much sense, and probably won't work very well for you. What works for me might not work for you, and it might not be good.

Anna: So are you saying it's not a good idea to copy other people?

Sally: I think sometimes other people's ideas are helpful, but at other times it's much more useful to just find out a bit about one another. Like if I were to help you to build a house, you could just copy mine, but we would have a much better time if we spent a time sharing what we both liked, and if I spend time hearing who you are and what you like.

Anna: (Laughing) Yes. You might live in a mansion, and not realize that I'm totally obsessed with Tiny Houses!

Sally: Is that one of the things you research when you're feeling your best?

Anna: Yes. I hope I might build one, one day!

Sally: Is studying about building Tiny Houses a Wellness Tool for you?

Anna: It surely is.

Discussion Topics

What does mutuality mean to you?

Do you feel that Peer Support relationships have to be mutual? Why or why not?

Have there been times when you felt a relationship was not mutual and then it changed so that it did feel mutual? If so describe that situation. Why did that happen? How did it feel when it happened? What was the result?

Could you have a Peer Support relationship with someone who was paid to provide Peer Support and you were not being paid? How do you think a situation like that could be handled so that it would work?

Hope

Hope is key to both WRAP and Peer Support. It is one of the Key Concepts of my recovery work and is included in the Values and Ethics of WRAP and Peer Support described in Chapter 6. In my early research, back in the late 1980s, I discovered that people who felt hopeful about their future were able to more easily move forward in their lives. When people have been dealing with mental health issues, and have been immersed in the mental health system, they may have a lot of fear, fear that gets in the way of hope. They may have been told, like I was, that they would never get better and would probably get worse over time. They may fear the side effects of the medications. They may be afraid they will get into situations where they will experience coercion, restraint or seclusion. While Peer Support can't promise to take away those fears, when the focus is on learning and working together, you can have *hope* that the results will move you toward what you want your life to be like.

Hope comes from being and working together, and knowing that, even though you may be uncomfortable with a difficult situation, you have hope that something interesting or even positive will come out of your experience. You may not know what it is, but gradually you begin to know that there is something to be learned from your discomfort and that there is hope. This creates possibilities that give you options, options that didn't exist when your goal was just to get by, before you had Peer Support.

Discussion Topics

Do you think having hope is important to Peer Support and moving forward? If so, why? If not, why not? Describe times when Peer Support has helped you stay hopeful, even in the hardest of times.

What makes it hard to be hopeful? What gives you a sense of hope? How does Peer Support help you to be hopeful?

Discussion Topics

How does it feel to describe yourself as you really are? What can you learn from that? What can others learn from that? How does that sharing increase feelings of mutuality?

Activity

People take turns describing themselves to others as they really are, as best they can. Each person will choose what they share about themselves. Discuss how that enhances mutuality.

Connection and Disconnection

Feeling connected to another person or a group of people is a special experience. In my view, it doesn't happen nearly enough. I am not sure anyone could get too much of it. When you feel connected to others, you feel comfortable, safe, relaxed and self-assured. This feeling of connection helps people feel hopeful and work on moving forward. It enhances Peer Support. Being listened to closely, validation and acceptance often increase feelings of connection.

Have you ever been in a conversation with someone and suddenly you felt a disconnect? Perhaps you felt like you weren't being heard, like the other person didn't understand, like they had some negative feelings toward you, like they were rejecting you in some way, or that you felt blamed or shamed, or even not smart enough. That is a disconnection. When this happens to me, I notice that a heavy feeling comes over me and I don't want to continue the conversation. Sometimes I feel like I just want to get away from the other person or people. I notice that I feel sad or angry about it for some time—there have been times when it was so serious I never again reconnected with the other person, or I avoided them.

Recently I have been trying to handle disconnection differently. When I feel a *disconnect*, I talk with the other person about it to see if we both had the same feeling or understood what happened, and to see if we could talk about it and get past it so that we could continue to have a mutual relationship that we both enjoyed.

Statements that usually support connection and those that often don't:

Supports connection
I would like to start on time. How could we make that happen?

Doesn't support connection
Why are you always late? It makes me really mad.

Supports connection
Could we start on time so I can leave in time to catch the bus?

Doesn't support connection
How come you guys don't ever start on time?

Supports connection
I need some time alone.

Doesn't support connection
I'm sick of everyone.

Supports connection
That doesn't sound right to me.

Doesn't support connection
You never tell me the truth.

Supports connection
Could we try another way of talking together?

Doesn't support connection
You are just a jerk.

Following is a list of things that can cause disconnection:

Sarcasm—cutting or bitter comments that make the other person feel bad.

Example: *Yeah, you'll do great job. You always were a big talker!*

Reminding the other person of painful past experiences—reminding the other person of things they have done in the past that have not worked out well or that they may feel badly or embarrassed about, rather than talking about what is happening now or something in the past that worked well.

Hurtful labels—There is no place in Peer Support for hurtful labels such as stupid, lazy, good-for-nothing, brat, fool or jerk.

Negative comparisons—comparing one person to another person in a negative way.

Example: *If only you were as smart as Jack.*

Threats—telling someone you are going to hurt them in some way. Sometimes people threaten other people as a way of trying to get them to do something they don't want to do.

Judgmental "you" messages—Speaking to the other person in an accusatory way.

"One-upmanship" or "Can you top this" stories—following someone's story by saying something like, "You think that was bad, wait until you hear what happened to me," or "My story is worse (or better) than that."

Activity

List or share with a Peer Supporter or group of Peer Supporters statements that usually support connection. Think of statements that might cause disconnection. Record these statements on labeled sheets of easel pad paper.

Discussion Topics

What does "connection" mean to you? How do you feel when you feel connected to another person or a group of people? Describe times when you felt connected to other people. What factors enhanced the feelings of connection?

What does "disconnection" mean to you? Describe times when you felt "disconnected" from another person or a group of people. How did that feel to you? Were you able to resolve the situation so that you felt connected again? If so, how did you do that? If you chose not to reconnect, why did you make that choice? Do you think it was the right choice? Why or why not?

Role Plays

Role-play a discussion that increased feeling of connection.

Role-play a situation that might create a feeling of disconnection.

Things you can do to Increase Connection in Peer Support

1. Treat everyone with dignity, compassion and respect at all times.
2. Accept other people as they are. Avoid trying to change them.
3. Consider varying perspectives, options and choices—avoid absolutes.
4. Avoid nagging.

5. Avoid responding out of your own impatience, anxiety or irritability.
6. Avoid, or have an agreed upon limit, to giving advice.
7. Respect other people's choices, stories, experiences and how they choose to spend their time.
8. Listen, listen, and listen, carefully and thoughtfully. Put limits around listening time when you need to.
9. Take really good care of yourself.
10. Avoid overwhelming the other person or people with information and detail. Summarize when you can.
11. Use "I" statements.
12. Avoid people who treat you badly.
13. Avoid sharing the detail of traumatic stories that may be upsetting to others and should be shared with a counselor.
14. Avoid all kinds of physical and emotional abuse.
15. Avoid teasing, bullying, and "put-downs."
16. Respect other people's boundaries
17. Keep a good sense of humor.
18. Respect the privacy of others.

Boundaries

As in all of life, boundaries or limits in relationships are important in Peer Support. Even though we might not think of some things as boundaries, they exist in all of our relationships. Not disturbing people when they are sleeping and giving people privacy in the rest room are examples of boundaries or limits that we experience every day and often don't even think about. In Peer Support, you have boundaries that will help assure that the relationship works for everyone and that you will be able to use your time together to share, learn and move forward in your lives.

In Peer Support, you may want to set limits or boundaries around things like:

- The amount of time you spend together

- Where time together is spent
- Whether or not you get together at other times, or have social time that is not peer support
- The things you discuss
- Time and number of phone calls or electronic communications
- Giving advice
- Connections with each other's family members, partners and friends
- The amount of physical touch

Boundaries differ from person to person. You can figure out what your boundaries are with each other, and if and when you want to change them, using Peer Support.

In Peer Support, as in all of life, you have the right to:

- Define your own limits and boundaries.
- Spend your time the way you choose.
- Feel comfortable and safe.
- Ask, expect and insist that others respect your physical boundaries.
- Protect yourself from unwanted closeness and contact.
- Determine how and by whom you want to be touched.
- Say "no" to anything you don't want to have happen to you or to do.
- Ask for what you need, want and deserve for yourself.

Sometimes people purposefully or unintentionally violate boundaries. You can deal with these situations by:

1. Telling the other person or people how you feel, and reminding them of your boundaries. You could discuss it using Peer Support. In a WRAP Group the "Comfort Agreement" (see Guidelines for WRAP and Peer Support in Chapter 8) can be used to address boundary issues.
2. If other people won't stop violating your boundaries, you can choose to discontinue the Peer Support relationship or drop out of the group.

Role Play

Two people are discussing the boundaries or limits they want in their Peer Support relationship.

Discussion Topics

What boundaries do you want to have in Peer Support? In WRAP Groups?

Share the boundaries in your lives. How do they work for you? Why are they important to you? If they are not important to you, why not?

How should boundary violations be handled?

Describe times when your boundaries worked well for you. Describe times when you had to negotiate with someone around boundaries, or had to end relationships because of boundary issues.

The next chapter describes the process of Peer Support, what it is like to be with another person and do the things described in the previous chapters.

Chapter 5

The Peer Support Process

While there is a predictable process that is commonly used to develop a Wellness Recovery Action Plan, a process that is clearly described in the Evidence-based Practice model and in the various WRAP resources, no such predictable process can exist for Peer Support. Peer Supporters figure it out as they go along. This chapter describes some of the options that can be part of Peer Support.

First Contact

The time when people first meet as Peer Supporters, *First Contact*, is key. It needs to be reassuring and supportive for everyone. As with all of Peer Support, since everyone's experience and situation is different, it is difficult to have clear guidelines around First Contact. Everyone involved may be feeling apprehensive, shy, scared and worried that this might not work, might not be right for you, or not right for the other person or people. One, both or several of you may have had limited contact with other people, perhaps for a very long time. You may never have had opportunities to discuss things in a supportive way with other people.

You may begin by introducing yourselves to each other, perhaps "pass pleasantries," talk briefly about the weather, difficulties getting there, where you will be meeting. In the ideal world, the people who are getting together for Peer Support would have decided for themselves that this is what they wanted to do, and perhaps even arranged it. That would make First Contact easier. If the person is in a facility or a program and was not told in advance that the Peer Supporter was coming to meet with them (not the best situation), the Peer Supporter could describe who he or she is, and briefly describe their experience in the mental health system. They might say, "I was a patient here last year. That is where I learned about Peer Support. It worked for me and I still use it. I am looking forward to Peer Support with you. I always learn so much." The other person might express surprise that the Peer Supporter expects to learn from their time together, rather than being there to tell her or him what to do. Depending on the situation, a Peer Supporter may want to share the Values and Ethics Handout in Appendix 1, and talk about any that seem confusing.

One of the Peer Supporters can begin by asking questions that might be as simple as "How are you doing?" "What's up?" "What's happened?" or "What's happening?" This scenario is probably different from what happened when people first reached out for other kinds of assistance and support. They may have been asked to fill out various forms that included personal information that they may not have felt ready to share, information about medications and previous treatment. They may have had to wait, first for an appointment, and then again when they arrived to get what they hoped would be "help."

If it is a WRAP Group, participants can chat with each other as they arrive. Then the group can start with an icebreaker (a simple activity that encourages interaction), led by the Facilitators. Then the Facilitators use the guidelines in this book to lead the group through the process of developing a WRAP.

Example of First Contact that led to Peer Support:
Jason had been on the mental health ward for two weeks. Sam was a Peer Supporter hired by the hospital. He stopped in to visit with Jason. Jason was not expecting him and was having a hard time getting going for the day. He was tired of the groups and resented the restrictive hospital atmosphere. Sam introduced himself and told Jason that he was a Peer Supporter who had had experiences similar to his in his life. He said he had even been a patient at that hospital and at several of the other local hospitals. He said that he was hired by the hospital to support patients because it works for people. Jason said he was sick of everything about the hospital and wasn't sure he was interested in talking to one more new person. Sam said that was OK but that it would be great if they could have at least a few minutes together because he always finds that he learns something new, something that moves him forward in his own life, each time he gets together with someone who has had experiences like his. Jason agreed that they could visit for a few minutes. Sam asked him what had been happening in his life before he came to the hospital. Jason told him his partner had left but was continuing to harass him. Sam said that sounded terrible and asked him how he was dealing with it. Jason said that was the problem. He didn't know how to deal with it and so he got more and more discouraged. And that is what brought him here. Sam asked if being in the hospital was helping him figure out how to get over the loss of his partner

and dealing with the harassment. He said he was getting a little help from the groups but not much really. Sam said that he once dealt with a co-worker who was harassing him and it really got him down. He said he talked to his boss about it and his boss told the other person he would be fired if it didn't stop. He asked Jason if there was anyone he could ask to tell his ex-partner to stop. He told Jason that a friend of his had actually gotten a lawyer to contact the person. Jason said he couldn't afford a lawyer but that he did know a legal aid lawyer who might help.

Discussion Topics

What do you think First Contact should be like in Peer Support? What do you think First Contact should be like with a WRAP Group Facilitator? What do you think First Contact should be like with other participants in the WRAP Group?

Share experiences with First Contact and how they felt to you. What was positive about these experiences? What could have been improved?

How do you feel about using "ice breakers" to help people feel comfortable in WRAP Groups? Describe any icebreakers that helped you feel more comfortable in a WRAP Group.

What's Next?

So you have made First Contact. Or you are getting together again after having met before. Now what happens? You have lots of options.

Listening

One of the choices you have in Peer Support is listening. In Peer Support, "really" listening to what the other person is saying gives us a broader and deeper understanding. Your silence as you listen is often the greatest gift that you can give another person. It gives them the opportunity to figure out for themselves what they want and need to do. I have often found that when I share something, something that may have been going around and around in my mind for a long time, with someone else, the next steps become readily apparent.

Listening requires you to be fully present—not distracted, not thinking about something else, and not thinking about how you're going to respond. If you can't listen or pay attention because you are too tired, too hungry, or distracted for any reason, let the other person know, and set up another time to get together.

Depending on the situation, I sometimes like to let the other person know how much time I have to listen and pay attention. I might say, "I can be here with you for half an hour and then I have to go pick up my children."

A Special Note

Our society is so fast-paced that we often don't take the time to listen. Do you have time to listen? Do you have time to really focus on the other person, instead of thinking about how you are going to respond, what story you are going to tell? Do you have time to wait for someone to get their words out, to think of what they are going to say? Do you have time to listen to someone who may stutter or who has a speech issue? Do you have time to wait while someone uses a text to speech device? Do you have time to be there for others?

Is speech the only way we can be there for others and show support? Can you take the time to write something out for someone who can't hear? Can you be there for people who can't speak, can't hear, or can't write? We interrelate by connection—with ourselves, the people in our lives, and the people on the planet we may think we have nothing in common with.

Remember Annie Sullivan, who taught Helen Keller how to communicate by making shapes in her palm. Do you have time to do that—to really connect with each other? To me, it is worth it.

For more ideas on Peer Support, where alternate ways of listening and communicating are necessary or might facilitate Peer Support, search on the Internet for "Augmentative and Alternative Communication."

Activity

Role play a situation where a person is describing him or herself as a "mental patient" and, by sharing some of your own experience, you learn more about them as a person. What can each of you learn from that?

Discussion Topics:

How do you know when someone is paying close attention and listening to you?

How does it feel to have someone pay close attention to you?

How does it feel to pay close attention to someone else?

How do you put limits around how much you can pay attention?

Have you ever deferred to someone else's need to be heard and not been heard yourself? How did that feel? What did you learn from that experience?

Activity

Two people take turns, 10 minutes each, paying attention to each other and listening to each other. Follow this time by discussing how that felt and what you might do differently another time.

Four or five people take turns, each person having 5 or 10 minutes, to share anything they want to share, or to express any feelings they want to feel. Follow this time with a time when each person shares how it felt to be paid attention to by the other people in the group.

Validation

Validation is a powerful Peer Support tool. Validation means saying supportive things that let the other person know you've heard them and understand. You can do this by saying something like: "That sounds really tough. You must be really strong to...," "After what you've been through, no wonder you feel angry/sad/afraid," "That must have been terrible," "Wow, that is wonderful", or "Congratulations." I have been deeply affected by validation when I shared something that was important to me and realized the other person understood what I was saying and why it was so important to me.

Discussion Topics

What does validation mean to you?

What are some statements that make you feel validated?

How does validation make you feel?

Why do you think validation is important?

Share times when you were validated and it made a difference to you.

Activity

Two people do a role-play. One person talks for 3 minutes about a difficult time they are having. Then they both talk about how they could validate the person who was talking. Then the other person takes a turn talking, followed by a similar discussion. People in a group share validating statements. These are recorded on easel pad paper and copies are made for participants.

Questions

Questions help the Peer Supporter understand the other person's perspective, what their experience has been in the past and their current experience. What would help you understand their perspective? How will you get a sense of the "big picture"? Questions like these that follow might deepen understanding for everyone involved and open opportunities for learning together:

"I wonder how you decided to …"

"Can you help me understand why that's meaningful for you?"

"Have you ever wondered how you learned to think that way?"

"Was there something that happened that made you do that?"

"Have you always felt that way?"

"Is there anything you could do instead when something like that happens?"

"Are there Wellness Tools you have used to get through hard situations?"

"Do you think WRAP has been responsible for all these good years?"

"Your motivation is impressive. What keeps you motivated?"

For example:

Joan says: "When you said that, it sounds like you believe that you are just a mental patient who can't think for herself. Is that true or am I hearing you wrong?" Serena says: "No, you are right. I think about myself as a mental patient who is not very smart. I feel like I have to depend on the doctors and case managers to tell me what to do." Joan says: "I used to believe that about myself too. Sometimes I still do. But now I know I can think for myself and have made lots of good decisions that have helped me move forward and even helped me to get a job that I enjoy. Do you think you could understand that you are smart and can make decisions about your own life?" Serena says, "I think it would be a stretch. Let's talk more about what that would look like."

Discussion Topic

How do you think questions can deepen understanding and make learning easier? Are there times when questions should not be asked?

Activity

People share questions they might ask in Peer Support. They are recorded on an easel pad and copies are made for each participant.

Say Back in Your Words What You Think You are Hearing

Saying back in your own words what you think the other person is telling you can help assure that you understand what they are trying to say. Sometimes language and emotions are hard to read. For example, if someone tells you that they are being "encouraged" to increase their medication at a time when they've been thinking about decreasing it, you might say, "Are you saying that you feel misunderstood?" If a person says they are looking for a different doctor, you could say, "Are you saying that you are uncomfortable with the doctor you have now?"

Discussion Topics

How do you think saying something back to a person in your own words helps? Do you think there might be times when it would not be helpful?

What can you learn together by saying things back to another person in your own words?

Describe situations in your own life when someone else repeated back in their own words what they thought you were saying. How did that work for you? How did it feel to you?

Activity

A person shares with another person an incident or experience. Then the other person repeats it back in his or her own words. They then discuss how that worked for them. Then they switch roles and repeat the exercise.

Share Personal Stories

In Peer Support, people often share part or all of their personal story. Peer Support may be the first time they have had this opportunity to share their story in a situation where they are not being analyzed or judged. People tell their stories in certain ways, based on their life experience, who they are talking to and who's listening. They may use their story to impress, to shock, to distance themselves from others, or to build mutual understanding and relationship and to figure out how to move forward. You are hearing the story based on your relationship with that person as a Peer Supporter and what is happening in their lives at the time. In Peer Support, you are only hearing one version of the story. Never disagree with another person's version of their story. This is their reality and is important and significant to them.

When two or more people begin to have a Peer Support relationship, they have no idea of the other person's lived experience, and how that lived experience has and is affecting their life, the choices they make and the things they do. As you share your stories, you can begin to see similarities and differences in your experience. You can think together about what the experience means, things you have learned from your experience and how, given your life experience, you want to and can move forward.

Discussion Topics

How do you think sharing stories supports mutual relationships and learning together?

Are there times when sharing stories is not OK? If so, when?

Are there stories that should not be told? If so, what are they?

Share times when you told your story and someone disagreed with you. How did that feel to you? What could that person have said that would help to move both of you forward?

Activity

People share stories and discuss responses to stories and what they learned from each other.

Responding

Validation, questions, sharing personal stories, and repeating things back in your own words are all ways of responding in Peer Support. The greatest challenge for me in Peer Support is making a choice about how to respond. I want my response to support mutuality, learning together, giving each other a sense of hope, and moving us both forward. There are no clear rules for how you respond. Over time you get more and more comfortable with it.

Activity

Responding takes practice. After talking with peers, reflect on how your responses felt. Reflection is described later in this chapter. Did they give a sense of hope? Did they support learning together? Did they move each of you forward in some way?

Discussion Topics

How do you think you can learn together by responding thoughtfully? What do you think that means?

How would it feel to be described as a mental patient?

How would it feel to be described as a schizophrenic?

Reflection

Take the time to reflect on how Peer Support is working for you and the other people involved by discussing how it felt after each time you spend together. Note any changes you want to make and things you want to do differently. During and after Peer Support sessions it can be useful to: 1. Talk with each other about what was helpful in your time together, 2. What worked, and 3. What was not helpful. Each session becomes a learning experience. You may notice over time how much better you feel, as you understand how to be effectively and mutually supportive with each other.

For instance, in reflecting on a WRAP Group, Charlotte described how badly she felt when a Peer Supporter told her that she shouldn't be having a beer every night with dinner and that she must be an alcoholic. She said she wished the other person had not jumped to the conclusion that she was an alcoholic and instead asked her for more information or how it made her feel.

Discussion Topics

What does reflection mean? How can it be helpful after Peer Support?

Share times when you felt that you were misunderstood and wished you had an opportunity to explain yourself.

Role Play

Two people spend 5 minutes, each describing how they respond to Triggers (or any other topic). Then they reflect on how that exchange worked for them.

Things that get in the way of Peer Support

Advice

Lots of people like to give advice. You may be used to giving lots of advice and you might feel that it is helpful. However, Peer Support is about learning together, not about giving advice. It is about working things through so you come up with ideas and solutions that will work. One person giving all the advice is the opposite of mutuality.

For example: A person comes to you and says that they're having lots of uncomfortable side effects from their medications but are afraid to tell their psychiatrist. Rather than telling them what you think they should do, giving them advice, you might say, "Boy, there was a time when I was feeling tired all the time from my medications. I couldn't get anything done. At that time I was afraid of my psychiatrist because he'd hospitalized me in the past, but I realized that not saying anything kept me in a place that I didn't want to be in."

When I first met my husband, we both got in the habit of giving each other lots of advice. And we noticed that all this "advice giving" was getting in the way of our relationship. We were feeling irritated with each other much of the time. Through talking it through we realized what was happening. We made a deal with each other that we would limit our advice to one piece of advice a day. We worked hard at it, and became better and better at keeping our advice to ourselves and instead discussing issues when they came up to find a solution that would work for both of us.

Discussion Topics

Share times when you gave advice to others and how it worked out. Do you think that you could have handled the situation a different way and had a better outcome, one that supported mutuality and learning together?

Share times when other people gave you advice and how that felt. If you wish they had done it another way, how do you wish they had handled the situation?

Assumptions

As a Peer Supporter, it is easy to make assumptions about what the other person is thinking or feeling and misread the situation. For example someone might be telling you that they are being evicted from their apartment. You may assume that they are worried about where they will be living and afraid of the future, but they are feeling really ashamed of not being able to pay their rent. If it is not clear what a person is feeling or sharing, you can say, "tell me more" or ask them questions like, "How did that make you feel? How are you feeling now?" Making assumptions about what other people are feeling can lead to misunderstandings and even feelings of disconnection. If you are not sure about the situation, ask for clarification and ask a lot of questions.

Discussion Topics

What does assumption mean to you?

Share times when others have made assumptions about you and how that felt. How did you handle it? Do you think you did it well, or would you do it differently another time?

Judgments

Like assumptions, people commonly make judgments about what other people are thinking, feeling or doing. Again, as with assumptions, avoid making judgments. As a Peer Supporter, we do not judge the other person, even if they are sharing something that we don't believe they should have done, or that they should do. Instead, ask more questions so that both of you develop a deeper understanding of the situation, learn together and move forward. For instance, Jill told Peter that she was thinking about getting a tattoo. She said that a lot of her friends were getting tattoos and she felt that it would help her fit in. Peter wanted to respond by saying something like, "Getting a tattoo is really dangerous" or "Why would you want to do a stupid thing like that?"—questions that would likely end the discussion of the topic or cause a disconnection. Instead he asked her questions like how she thought it would feel if she fit in and if there were other things she was doing as well to feel more comfortable with others.

Discussion Topics

How do you think you should handle it if someone is talking about doing something that you think is not a good idea?

Have you judged people in the past? What were the results? How would you handle the situation another time?

Describe times when you have judged other people and the results.

Describe times when others have judged you, how it felt and how you responded.

There is no end to learning about Peer Support, and there is no limit to what we can accomplish in Peer Support. As you practice Peer Support, if you discover things that you feel other people should know, that will help them be more effective Peer Supporters, write about them and send them to info@WRAPandRecoveryBooks.com.

Chapter 6

Values and Ethics of WRAP and Peer Support

As people began using WRAP and Peer Support more and more, particular values and ethics grew up around them, values and ethics that the people who used them felt were key to success.

The following WRAP and Peer Support Values and Ethics are not specific to WRAP and to Peer Support. They can serve as a guide to successful relationships and successful living in all of life. If everyone followed them in all of their interactions with each other, what an amazing and wonderful place this world would be. We can begin to do that right now, each of us.

> *Immerse yourself in these Values and Ethics—talk about them, think about them, do role-plays with peers, until they become the way you* ***always*** *do things in all of your life.*

These Values and Ethics were developed over time, over a very long time, by peers, by people providing input and feedback because they wanted to move forward in their own lives, and they wanted to support that movement forward in the lives of others. They were not a mandate from some higher authority, but rather evolved as people considered what was important to them and revised them again and again. They can still be revised and updated at any time that a significant number of people suggest that should happen.

You can help assure that these values become your guide in relationships and in all aspect of your life if you discuss each of them with individual peers and in Peer Support groups, WRAP Groups and WRAP support groups, and practice using them in these situations.

Hope

> *WRAP Groups and WRAP and Peer Support focus on* ***hope.*** *There are numerous studies that have shown that people who have mental health challenges, and all kinds of life issues, recover and move on with their lives. They get well, stay well for long periods of time, and do the things they want to do with their lives. There is lots of hope.* ***The old messages that told us we could never recover, that we would get worse over time, and that there is nothing we can do to help ourselves, were wrong.*** *If others say things like this to us, we should tell them that it is not helpful and that we want only support that is encouraging and hopeful.*

Example that is *Not Hopeful*:

Joan tells Mary that she is feeling discouraged. She said that when she was working on her WRAP in her WRAP Group, she decided she could go back to school, something she had always wanted to do. She says her doctor told her that she was mentally ill, that she would never get any better and that she would probably get worse over time. She said that he told her to stop trying to go back to school. Mary said that she should just get used to it and stop thinking about going back to school because it just wouldn't be possible for her. Joan leaves feeling discouraged and not knowing what to do next.

Example that is *Hopeful*:

Joan tells Mary that she is feeling discouraged. She says that when she was working on WRAP in her WRAP Group, she decided to go back to school, something she had always wanted to do. Her doctor told her that she was mentally ill, that she would never get any better and that she would probably get worse over time. He said she could never go back to school. Mary says her doctor told her that, too, and it made her feel awful. "But," she says, "I have read that people who have mental health challenges do recover and move on with their lives, that it has been proven in many different studies." She says when her doctor told her that she would never get better and would probably get worse over time, it made her even more determined to finish her education and get the job she wanted, which she did. She said she would be glad to support Joan in doing that. She asked Joan what would be the next step in moving forward with her plans. Joan said she needed to apply for financial aid but that the forms were baffling to her. Mary said she had difficulty with them, too, but had gotten them figured out, and offered to help Joan with them.

No one, no matter how educated they are or the position they hold, has the right to predict the course of our future, or of our life, or to take action that would prevent us from being who we want to be.

Discussion topics

Define hope.

What gives you a feeling of hope?

What takes away hope?

Why is hope so powerful?

When have you felt most hopeful?

What do you hope for?

When have others tried to take away your hope? How have you responded when this happened? How might you respond if it happened again?

Self-determination, personal responsibility, empowerment, and self-advocacy are key components of WRAP, Peer Support, and WRAP and Peer Support together.

Even though you are working with a Peer Supporter, or in a WRAP or Peer Support group, **it is always your choice about what you include in your WRAP and what you do moving forward in your life**. That is **self-determination**. In other kinds of mental health and health care programs, you may not have **self-determination**. Your rights to self-determination may have been taken away. You may have been expected to follow the orders of other people, even though you know it won't be helpful, or may even be harmful.

Self-Determination Discussion Topics

What does self-determination mean to you?

Right now, are you able to determine the course of your own life? If not, what gets in the way? What could you do to change that?

Describe times when you have made decisions about your own life and how that worked for you—what was hard, what worked well.

Describe things that you would include in your WRAP if it were "all up to you." Share the circumstances that are keeping those things from happening and ideas of things you could do that might change that dynamic.

Given self-determination, it is our **personal responsibility** to do what we want and need to do for ourselves and to accept the consequences for things that did not work out well. The hard part of **personal responsibility** can be motivation. You may have been in the "system" for a long time. You may have lived in an institution for an extended period of time. You may still be living in an institution or living in a situation where you are told what to do and what not to do. Living in circumstances like that makes it hard to feel motivated to do anything. You will get better and better at taking personal responsibility with practice and over time. WRAP and Peer Support will be your guide as you move forward.

Personal Responsibility Discussion Topics

Do you feel like you take personal responsibility for your own life? If so, how do you do that? If not, how could you take more personal responsibility for your own life?

Do you think you would be more satisfied with your life if you took more responsibility for it? If so, why? If not, why not?

Describe times when you have taken personal responsibility and how it has worked for you.

Self-Advocacy

Often people who are entrenched in a care system or who live with people who make their decisions for them and always do things for them, don't know how to advocate for themselves. Through the process of developing a WRAP with Peer Support, and using Peer Support as you take back control of your life, you will learn self-advocacy skills and strategies. You may want to role-play with your peers, to practice advocating for yourself before you have to do this with someone you don't know, or someone who thinks they should be in control of you and can make better decisions for you than you can make for yourself.

Role Play ideas (you can think of many more):

Asking your doctor to reduce a medication that is causing you to have uncontrollable movements

Seeking financial aid to go back to school

Getting an apartment that is safe and better meets your needs

Asking someone to stop bullying or teasing you

Asking someone to keep someone else from treating you badly

Ending a relationship with an abusive partner

In all WRAP Groups, Peer Support groups and related programs, everyone is *equal* and the relationships we have with each other are mutual. Everyone leaves their "hat" or title at the door and participates in the process as *equals*. Doctors, case managers, people who have had health difficulties for years—all are equal in WRAP Groups, treating each other with mutual respect while learning together. That means that even if you have been in an institution for many years, if you have a hard time learning, have little money or education, or if you are a psychiatrist with years of training and experience, or are very wealthy, you are treated with the same dignity, compassion, mutual respect, and unconditional high regard, as unique, special individuals, including complete acceptance of diversity with relation to culture, ethnicity, language, religion, race, gender, age, disability, sexual identity, and "readiness" issues.

In WRAP Groups, you can use the "Comfort Agreement," described in more detail in Chapter 8, Guidelines for Using WRAP and Peer Support Together, to help assure that all participants are treated as *equals*.

Discussion Topics

If you are a WRAP Facilitator, what can you do to make sure everyone who attends feels like an "equal" and that relationships between people in the group are mutual? Describe situations where you were treated well and how that made you feel. Describe situations where you were not treated with dignity, compassion and respect, and how that made you feel.

Do you feel that you have a hard time treating some people with dignity, compassion and unconditional high regard? If so, why? What would you like to do about it?

How do you respond when people treat you badly? Do you think a different response might be more effective? If so, what would that be?

How can you help assure that Peer Support relationships are mutual?

There are "no limits" to recovery. In WRAP and Peer Support groups and in working with each other as peers, no one tells us what we can or can't do or what we can achieve in our lives. I can remember being told that I would never get better, that I would get worse over time and that, since they don't keep people like me in institutions any more, my adult children would have to provide me with care for the rest of my life. I was told it was time for me to give up my dreams of more education, a career, owning my own home and having a loving relationship. I was told I could never write a book or lead a workshop. Since that time I have gotten master's and doctor's degrees, have built a successful career and business, have written twenty-five published books, have led many, many workshops, have owned my home and have been happily married for the last twenty years. Suppose I had believed what they had told me! In WRAP and Peer Support groups, we don't make predictions about people or tell them what they can and can't do. We listen to what they want and plan to do. Then we encourage and support them as they move forward in their lives in whatever way they choose. WRAP and Peer Support are tools to facilitate this process, to think about possibilities, to make plans, and to implement plans.

Role Play

A situation where you have told a peer that you want to become a successful musician and want to figure out how to do it

A situation where someone is telling you that you can't get more education because you have mental health issues

Discussion Topics

Share success stories about being given advice that was different than what you wanted to do, how you responded to that advice and the eventual outcome.

Discuss "no limits to recovery" and how it affects you in your life.

Every aspect of WRAP and Peer Support is voluntary. The person who is developing their WRAP decides if they want to do it, when they want to do it, how long they will take, what it will include, who assists and supports them in the process and whether they will use Peer Support to enhance the WRAP process.

How does it make you feel when someone tells you that you have to do something, that it is mandated? Does it make you feel more or less motivated? Most people would say that when they are told they must do something, they may do it, but they might not really want to and might not put a lot of effort into it. Peers agree that WRAP and Peer Support needs to be voluntary.

Discussion Topics

Why do you think WRAP and Peer Support should be voluntary?

How do you think WRAP and Peer Support would work if they were not voluntary?

The person who is developing their WRAP and using Peer Support is the only expert on herself or himself. **Who knows more about you than you know about yourself?** In your life, and as you have reached out for help with health and mental health issues, people may have told you that they know more about you than you know about yourself. That can't be true. There is no one who has your sleeping dreams and your waking dreams. There is no one who feels what you feel, sees what you see, hears what you hear. There is no one who knows how you feel when you feel lonely, or sad, or happy, or joyful. There is no one besides you who can be the expert on you.

When Peter was working on his WRAP with a Peer Supporter, he decided that he needed a new doctor. At his first visit with a doctor who he thought would work for him, the doctor told Peter that he knew what was best for him, that he was the expert, and he expected Peter to follow his recommendations without question. Peter decided that he would not stay with this doctor and went on to work successfully with a different doctor, who understood that Peter was the expert on himself.

Discussion Topics

How do you know that you are the expert on yourself? How does that feel to you? Do you think knowing that you are the expert on yourself will make it easier for you to advocate for yourself? Explain.

In WRAP and Peer Support, the focus is on personal strengths and away from perceived deficits. In working together, people focus on the things they do well, and avoid focusing on negative self-judgments or the findings of deficit-based assessments. There is research evidence that proves that a strengths-based approach supports recovery. When I was having mental health challenges many years ago, health care providers suggested that I have a battery of psychological tests. I agreed, took the tests and looked forward to the results, thinking that they would give me some insight that would be helpful. Imagine my disappointment when the results they shared were all things that they considered to be deficits, things like: has a hard time getting to know people, is not trusting, and should not consider further education. This was not helpful to me in any way and precipitated a deep depression. When I thought about the situation, I decided to ignore the results of the tests, and move forward with my educational and life plans.

Discussion Topics

How does it make you feel when you and others focus on your strengths?

How does it make you feel when you and others focus on your deficits?

Which approach would you prefer? Which approach do you think is most helpful?

What are your strengths? Where would you include them in your WRAP? How can Peer Support help you figure out your strengths?

Over and over, peers have said that they do not like clinical, medical, and diagnostic language, and that instead they would prefer to use words that describe what they feel. WRAP Facilitators and Peer Supporters avoid the use of labels and medical and diagnostic language as much as possible. Many people say it helps them to move forward when they describe how they really feel, rather than being put into some kind of category or given a diagnosis.

Jane's case manager told her that she had bipolar disorder and an anxiety disorder. This made Jane feel uncomfortable. She didn't really know what these words meant. When she looked them up, it became even more confusing. Some of the words seemed to describe her and her situation and some did not. Working together with a Peer Supporter, she found that words like sadness, irritable, thinking she could do impossible things, and spending too much money on things she didn't need, more accurately described how she was actually feeling. She then used these descriptive words to enhance her WRAP. First, Jane identified signs in the Early Warning Signs and When Things are Breaking Down parts of her WRAP. Then she used Wellness Tools to move forward so she could feel the way she wanted to feel and be the way she wanted to be.

Discussion Topics

How do you feel about diagnostic labels? How do they make you feel when they are about you?

How do you feel about medical language?

Role Play

One person, the doctor, gives the other person, the patient, a diagnosis of schizophrenia. The person tells the doctor how this makes him feel and asks the doctor to work with him to uncover what he is really experiencing and how he could respond to uncomfortable feelings using WRAP and Peer Support.

The emphasis is on the many different Wellness Tools that are simple and safe, and away from methods that are invasive or that may have serious, devastating, or long-lasting side effects.

As I began studying how people cope with mental health issues every day, and how they recover and move on with their lives, I was in awe of the many, many different things that I discovered people were doing for themselves on their own. This realization was the beginning of what eventually became the Wellness Toolbox. As I began to learn what was working for other people, I began looking closely at my own life and discovered many resources, free resources at my fingertips, that could support me through the worst of times, and that could enhance my life all the time. I now have a list of over 100 choices, Wellness Tools, which I can use for myself to walk me through hard times and make every day of my life rich and rewarding. When I have to reach out for more invasive choices, I know I can do that, but it is the simple, safe, non-invasive choices that sustain me, and that sustain so many of the people I have learned from.

People may choose to use some of the more "invasive" tools, like medications and electroshock, or even things like cutting and using alcohol. These are personal choices and are respected in Peer Support.

Activity

Make lists of all the things you do that keep you feeling well, that help you feel better when you are not feeling well, that you use to enrich your life, and that you do for fun. You can do this in a group, recording people's responses on a sheet of easel pad paper that can be posted on the wall. Groups often come up with very long lists. Discussing people's choices encourages them to "think outside the box," coming up with even more choices or tools. Someone could volunteer to input these lists in a computer and make copies for everyone so they can consider them when they are working on their own Wellness Toolbox and the other sections of WRAP.

Discussion Topics

Discuss in more depth any of the Wellness Tools that people share, and also those that are included in other WRAP resources like *WRAP for Life* (Copeland, M. 2014 Dummerston, VT: Peach Press). For other resources go to www.WRAPandRecoveryBooks.com.

Discuss controversial choices and Wellness Tools like cutting, alcohol and marijuana.

Difficult feelings and behaviors are normal responses to traumatic life circumstances, and are not a "symptom" or a diagnosis. This means that WRAP and Peer Support are trauma-informed.

Every one of us has had traumatic things happen to us in our lives. The effect of these traumatic incidents and their relationship to our difficult feelings and behaviors is becoming more and more widely recognized. As Peer Supporters working together to develop a WRAP, this needs to be recognized. *WRAP for the Effects of Trauma,* (Copeland, M. 2012 Dummerston, VT: Peach Press) and *Healing the Trauma of Abuse,* (Copeland, M. and Harris, M. 2000 Oakland, CA: New Harbinger Publications) have many ideas, tools and strategies for addressing trauma-related issues.

When working on WRAP using Peer Support, keep the focus on moving forward in our lives, even while recognizing that people have histories of trauma, acknowledging their stories, and accepting that these experiences of trauma affect the way people see themselves and the world. Some people find that sharing traumatic stories is not helpful in the group setting, or, depending on the situation, even when you are working together as Peer Supporters one-on-one. While validating another person's experience by saying something like "That is terrible, I am so sorry to hear that is happening to you," it is acceptable to tell someone that what they are sharing is hard to hear and would be best shared with someone else or a counselor.

WRAP Groups can sometimes get overwhelmed with people's stories. While acknowledging the significance and importance of these stories and the impact they have had on people's lives, people can keep the focus on the current task. Or you can include a statement in the Comfort Agreement that defines the kinds of things that can be discussed in the group, or how long a person can spend sharing their story.

Discussion Topics

How do you think the difficult things that have happened to you in your life are affecting you now? What would you like to change about that? What have you done to overcome the effects of trauma in your life?

Whenever possible, people work together and learn with peers, to increase mutual understanding, knowledge, and promote wellness.

This book is all about working together with peers as we recover, move forward in our lives and make our lives the way we want them to be.

Discussion Topics

What is Peer Support? What does it mean to you?

Do you think it is more effective to work with others as you develop your WRAP or to do it on your own? Explain your response.

Share ways that Peer Support has enhanced your life.

Share ways that Peer Support has helped you uncover more Wellness Tools and helped you develop a more effective and powerful WRAP.

Recovery is a process of change through which individuals improve their health and wellness, live a self-directed life, and strive to reach their full potential.

Chapter 7

WRAP and Peer Support Together

Both WRAP and Peer Support were developed in the mid 1990s by people with lived experience of mental health issues. Both grew from the "grassroots," from a desire to create lives and communities that inspired hope and possibility instead of being about illness, symptoms and problems. Both WRAP and Peer Support assume that we can make choices and take personal responsibility for ourselves and our future. The traditional, deficit-based services we were receiving were limiting and keeping us from moving forward in our lives, seeing ourselves as needy recipients with little hope for the future.

WRAP and Peer Support are being increasingly used and accepted by individuals, groups and providers around the world. While WRAP provides a concrete plan and pathway forward for an individual, Peer Support offers ways of supporting one another to do this in relationship and in communities. WRAP and Peer Support work well together and complement one another.

Anyone can develop a WRAP on their own. But many people will choose to create a WRAP with others. Many of us have begun our healing and moving forward after years of intense challenges in our lives. We may have had great difficulty being with and/or communicating with others and may have been misunderstood and marginalized. In addition, we may have lived in very isolated, impoverished circumstances at home, in the community or in an institution. Many of us were treated badly and were repeatedly traumatized, sometimes when we reached out for assistance and support. Many of us have never had the chance to develop healthy relationships. We may have forgotten how to relate to others, if we ever knew how to do this. Our model for helping relationships is often based on relationships with "professionals." Experience has shown that WRAP developed with Peer Support can be more comprehensive and effective, making it easier to get on with our lives.

WRAP and Peer Support:

- Have the same Values and Ethics.
- Can happen in places where people often gather (whether the context is mental health or something else), situations that provide opportunities for learning about WRAP and Peer Support.
- Becomes a personal journey supported and enhanced by others, rather than something imposed.
- Provides opportunities for supporting one another to implement WRAP, finding new ways to move through stress and crisis, and create the life of our choosing.
- Provides opportunities to challenge ourselves and each other about old ways of thinking and to create new ways of thinking.

Expected outcomes from the use of Peer Support and WRAP include:

- Deeper, more meaningful and rewarding relationships
- Improved quality of life
- Increased use of natural supports
- More support for developing personal responsibility
- Increased understanding of difficult or intense feelings and behaviors
- Decrease in the incidence of difficult or intense feelings and behaviors
- Decrease in the impact of traumatic life events and discrimination caused by difficult feelings and behaviors
- Decreased need for costly therapies and health services

The expected long term outcomes of WRAP and Peer Support are:

- A shift of focus away from 'symptom control' to moving forward in our lives.
- A potential reduction in the need for costly mental health and emergency services as we take responsibility for our own wellness and our own life, finding new ways to manage and reduce difficult feelings and behaviors using WRAP and Peer Support, and effectively reach out to a wide support

network, which might include peers, family members, friends and health care providers.

- An increased ability to meet life and career goals, significant life enhancement, and gains in self-esteem and self-confidence as we become contributing, valued members of the community.

Who Can Benefit from WRAP and Peer Support

Peer Support and WRAP are for anyone who wants to use them, regardless of their history, physical or mental health issues, diagnosis or treatment, or how capable other people believe them to be. Families, friends, health care providers, clinicians, and even the individuals themselves, are frequently surprised to find that in a connected mutual relationship, anybody can develop supportive relationships and a WRAP.

People have started their journeys when they were unable to speak or could only mutter, when they were hearing voices constantly, when they were having difficulty sitting still for even a moment, when they had not moved at all for a very long time, and when they had been diagnosed with any of the multitude of so-called psychiatric disorders and/or physical illnesses. And they've begun where they were, perhaps making only very small changes at first. People have taken their first steps and gradually, over time, taken back control of their lives, moved on to work toward meeting their personal aspirations and dreams, working with and encouraging others in the process.

Chapter 8

Guidelines for WRAP and Peer Support

Someone or several people may have heard about WRAP and want to work with others developing WRAP plans using Peer Support methods and strategies. Some of the options for preparing to work together include:

- Attending a basic WRAP seminar, series of classes or online classes
- Taking the Mental Health Recovery and WRAP Correspondence Course
- Attend a WRAP Facilitator training
- Attend a WRAP and Peer Support training or a Peer Support training.
- Taking the online WRAP One-on-One course and other online WRAP courses

If you want to work on WRAP using Peer Support, either as individuals or in groups, and neither you or the person or people you want to work with has been to the trainings, *work with what you already have!* You can read this book and other suggested resources, follow the processes that are described, and begin. Get the training as soon as you can but don't wait to start working with WRAP and Peer Support. The structure of WRAP, the guidelines for Peer Support, and the Values and Ethics of WRAP and Peer Support will guide you in the process.

As you move forward, get feedback from the other person or people that you are working with. The essence of both WRAP and Peer Support is people learning and moving forward together. If you are planning a group, it's ideal to have at least two people to share responsibility at the start. Ultimately, everyone in the group shares responsibility for the group.

If you are doing WRAP in a group, one or several people in the group who are familiar with WRAP may facilitate the group process using Peer Support as a framework. They describe each section of WRAP, share examples and get input from group members. The group could choose to take turns with facilitation, with different people being responsible for learning about a section and sharing it with the group. However the group chooses to work together, the group belongs to the group, not to the facilitator, and each group member shares equal responsibility for what happens in the group.

Most WRAP Groups use an easel, newsprint paper and markers to record input from people in the group. After each section of the plan is described, the people in the group share their ideas. These can be recorded on a sheet of newsprint paper, labeling the top of the sheet with the topic, like "Wellness Toolbox" or "Early Warning Signs." The list can be posted on the wall for easy reference during WRAP development. Someone in the group could volunteer to input the lists on a computer and print copies for everyone. Individuals can share their personal lists if they choose to.

In the past, people developed their WRAP in a *binder* with filler paper and a set of five tabs. These days more and more people are developing their WRAP on their computer or other electronic device. Some are using the "Build Your Own WRAP" program and/or the WRAP app. There are many books that describe various aspects of WRAP and most include WRAP forms in the back. There is a WRAP Workbook that contains the WRAP forms. Any kind of notebook or paper works as well. The person who is developing the WRAP decides what they will use.

WRAP plans are the personal property of the person who writes them. They are not to be kept by providers or anyone else. Our WRAP belongs to us personally and is not to be taken from us, reviewed or judged by anyone.

WRAP can be created in any order, in any time frame and can be changed at any time. Everything is optional. The WRAP format that is evidence-based, the one that the research has shown works, is described in all of the many WRAP resources, but you can do your WRAP any way you want to.

You could attend a WRAP and Peer Support session and never develop a WRAP or you could choose to just do part of the WRAP. WRAP is not mandatory or a compulsory, required part of a treatment or recovery plan. Some people find that it is helpful just attending the group or talking with someone about WRAP. Too often people have been taught that there is nothing they can do to help themselves. WRAP and Peer Support prove otherwise.

Any goal setting (if you choose to have goals) is done by the person whose goal it is. No goals are set for a person by others. There is no one in charge in

WRAP Groups or in developing a WRAP—everyone is in charge. Groups are led by facilitators who are trained to lead people through the WRAP process. Individuals working together on a WRAP are each in charge of every aspect of their own WRAP.

Agencies and organizations may want to have the "goal" that everyone who attends a WRAP Group develops a personal WRAP including a Crisis Plan. This is not the intention of WRAP. WRAP is voluntary. A person can come to a WRAP Group and choose to just sit through all the sessions without participating in any way. They may participate in some ways or not participate at all. Sometimes just being able to attend the group is a monumental achievement. If someone decides to set goals for themselves, that would be a personal decision, not a decision to be made by someone else.

Everyone involved in developing or revising a WRAP can give feedback and share information. No one is the "expert." Regardless of education, life experience, wealth or social status, WRAP Groups are places where everyone is treated as an equal, valued and contributing member. People can support each other by saying encouraging things like: "That sounds like an idea worth exploring. I wonder if there might be even more possibilities…", "When I was in a similar circumstance, this is what worked for me," "I wonder if you've thought of…" or "Can you think of any other ideas?"

Working together as individuals or as a group, even when focused on a common task like developing a WRAP, is not always easy. There is no one "right way."

Guidelines or Comfort Agreement

For people working together and for groups, it may help to develop together a list of guidelines or a "comfort" or even a "discomfort agreement" that guides the process of working. For groups, these guidelines can be posted for easy reference. This agreement is a way of setting up the environment to allow for risk-taking.

The agreement might include some of the following:

- Listen respectfully when others are sharing.
- Avoid sharing personal information about others outside of the session or group—keep all sharing confidential. Also, if it is particularly important to you that something be confidential, tell the group.

- Speak from your own experience, using language that reflects you, not the experience of others.
- Treat each other with dignity, compassion and respect.
- Keep cell phones off or on silent, and keep interactions with your phone or other electronic devices outside the room (unless you are note-taking).
- Speak one at a time.
- Take responsibility for your own needs.
- Avoid treating each other as fragile.
- Ask for what you need (including clarification).

These lists can be added to or changed when the people involved decide to do so.

The guidelines can be changed as the group works together. The group can keep referring back to them or tweaking them. Some of the issues that may need attention in groups are:

- People who talk too much without giving others a chance to speak
- Someone acting as if they are the expert on everything
- Interruption
- Someone wanting all the attention paid to their needs
- Joking that interferes with doing the work that others want to do
- Judgments of others
- Personal agendas (e.g., political or religious)

People who are working on their WRAP can choose to take time to share their life stories or discuss any topics that are mutually agreed upon.

Key Recovery Concepts

People who are using Peer Support to develop a WRAP often choose to begin by reviewing and discussing the Key Concepts. I discovered these Key Concepts when I first began studying how people cope with mental health issues and how they recover and move on with their lives. As I reviewed the masses of input I was getting from people everywhere, these Key Concepts began to emerge. In the many years that I have now been doing this work, these Key Concepts have remained constant. They provide the foundation of effective recovery work.

Hope—People who experience mental health difficulties get well, stay well and go on to meet their life dreams and goals.

Discussion Topic

What has helped you to feel hopeful?

Personal Responsibility—It's up to you, the person who is choosing to work toward recovery and wellness, with the assistance of others, to take action and do what needs to be done to move toward the life that you choose for yourself.

Discussion Topic

When have you successfully taken responsibility for your own wellness and your own life?

Education—Learning all you can about what you are experiencing and what your choices are, gives you the information you need to make good decisions about all aspects of your life.

Discussion Topics

How can you educate yourself about mental health challenges and issues, and about WRAP and about Peer Support?

Self-Advocacy—Effectively reaching out to others so that you can get what it is that you need, want and deserve to support yourself as you move forward in your life.

Discussion Topics

Describe times when you have successfully advocated for yourself. What makes self-advocacy hard?

Why do you think many people don't advocate for themselves?

Support—While working toward wellness is your personal responsibility, receiving support from others, and giving support to others, will support you in moving forward and enhancing the quality of your life.

Discussion Topics

What have you learned about support since you began working on WRAP and Peer Support?

How does it feel to be supported?

How can you use support as a Wellness Tool?

Section 2

Developing WRAP with Peer Support

Chapter 9

Wellness Toolbox

The Wellness Toolbox provides the underpinnings for WRAP. This is a list of the many simple, safe self-help resources you discover for yourself that help you stay well, as well as those that help you feel better. These could also be called strengths or assets. Many people don't see the things they do to help themselves as strengths or assets.

In a WRAP Group, the facilitators begin working on this section of WRAP by describing the concept of a Wellness Toolbox and Wellness Tools. They may show the group the PowerPoint slides that describe The Wellness Toolbox. They may also share some of their own Wellness Tools. Then they ask group members to share their Wellness Tools and someone records them on a sheet of posted easel pad paper. These lists can be entered into a computer, with copies given to each person in the group.

As this is happening, people may have comments or questions about specific tools, or even want to have longer discussions about certain tools. These valuable discussions can lead to further consideration, understanding and ideas. Sometimes there are constraints on how much time can be spent on this, constraints imposed by the needs of the group or by the sponsoring agency or organization. While it may not be possible, the ideal would be for these conversations to go on for as long as the people involved want to have them. This might mean that instead of spending an hour working on Wellness Tools, it might take two or three hours. The conversation could be continued another time, some people in the group might want to stay later, or they might meet separately to continue the conversation.

If people are working together one-on-one as peer supporters, it would be optimal to have the time to spend on this and other WRAP related issues be open-ended so that everything can be discussed in whatever depth is beneficial to both peers. People need to be clear about any time constraints they may have that will affect how much time they spend together working on these and other parts of WRAP.

Using Peer Support, people can consider and discuss some of the common Wellness Tools that are listed in the various WRAP resources (see Appendix) as well as others they have discovered, even those that they have thought about using but never tried. Some common Wellness Tools that others have shared in WRAP Groups and with each other using Peer Support, and online in response to Facebook queries, include:

Peer Support
Using social media
Video games
"Surfing" the net
Texting
Participating in an online support group
Discussing a difficult issue with another person
Expressing emotion (crying, yawning, shaking, screaming)
Relaxation exercises
Rest or Sleep
Eating healthy food (Describe what that means for you)
Drinking 8 glasses of water a day
Walking
Solitude
Meditation
Revising plans
Taking a break
Counting to 10 before responding
Telling someone how I feel
Avoiding certain people
Avoiding certain places

Using Peer Support, people can think together about new tools they might be willing to try. These might include trying something they didn't think they could do, or being really open and honest with a friend even when it's difficult. Depending on the situation, it may help to have time limits on certain activities. For instances, if a person took a half hour walk, that might be a good Wellness Tool. But if they walked 20 miles to a nearby town and their feet got all blistered, it might not be a good idea. If they worked on a writing project for several hours a day, it might be a good idea. But if they worked on it for days and days without sleeping, it might not be a good idea. They can think more deeply about these tools by discussing them with a peer or with peers in a WRAP Group.

These days many people are using technology and social media as Wellness Tools and as ways to get support. In the Appendix you will find a listing of responses to a query on Facebook about how people use social media as Wellness Tools. The tools they shared include:

The WRAP app
Facebook groups
Facebook secret groups
Facebook Messenger Apps
Having a personal page on Facebook
Twitter groups linking up and sharing ideas
Email
Skype
Facetime
Instagram
Snap Chat
Glide
Hangout
Texting
Phone calls
App "Optomism"
Using "emoticons"
Playing video games
Webinars
Podcasts
Online videos
Online movie services
"7 Cups of Tea" (a world-wide 24 hour Peer Support chat)
SMART Recovery
Warm line

You can discuss all of your collective resources as you work together either as individuals or in a WRAP Group, learning together as you think "outside the box," and outside of the usual mental health and health care framework.

Working together, as individuals one-on-one or in groups, people often come up with long lists of Wellness Tools. I have learned that when I am feeling badly or trying to keep myself well, there is always a simple, safe Wellness

Tool I can use. I used to reach for a medication or call a crisis line, but I don't do that anymore. One of the Wellness Tools I use most is Peer Support. I contact a friend, we talk about what I am experiencing and we share ideas on actions I might take. Sometimes my supporter encourages me to "think outside the box." Usually that is all I need to feel better.

Some people have actually developed a physical Wellness Toolbox: a basket, box, drawer or shelf where we keep Wellness Tools or reminders of Wellness Tools, things like a poetry book, a box of watercolors, massage lotion, a relaxation tape, a journal, etc. Another idea is hanging the list of Wellness Tools on the refrigerator or a bulletin board, or having a list of Wellness Tools on the bedside table for quick and easy reference. You can discuss these kinds of ideas with peer supporters.

Occasionally, someone finds the Wellness Toolbox concept, and the idea that they can use these simple, safe tools to help themselves, so useful that they don't choose to go any further with WRAP at the time. Others may just want to listen to the discussion and not write anything down. Talking with peers about these kinds of choices can enhance clarity—"should we do it that way or shouldn't we?"

Bob lives in prison. He will be there for several more years. He is working with some of his peers on developing a Wellness Toolbox for himself in anticipation of developing a WRAP, a challenging task for someone who is in prison and has limited options. Discussing this situation with others in the WRAP Group using Peer Support strategies helped him expand his list of options. Jack asked Bob what kinds of things worked for him before he was in prison. Bob thinks for a minute, laughs and says, all the kinds of things that landed him in prison. The group laughs and various people share how hard it has been to change some of their habits and thinking. Jack then says, it may sound stupid but that he always feels better when he keeps things in his very small personal space well organized and his bunk smoothed out. He also said a daily shower helps him a lot. Others joined in and were then able to add things to their list like staying away from trouble makers, taking advantage of educational opportunities like learning how to use a computer, going to groups that help pass the time even when they are not compelling, learning a foreign language, getting a high school diploma and even wearing a clean shirt.

Several weeks ago, Sarah, a volunteer peer supporter, began visiting Millie, who has been a patient at the state hospital for three years. Millie is 62 and has been a patient in psychiatric hospitals repeatedly over the years. She and Sarah have developed a mutually supportive relationship. Sarah has told Millie that she has developed a WRAP for herself and would like to work with Millie on developing a Wellness Toolbox and then the rest of WRAP, if Millie was interested in doing that. Sarah says that she herself has been having a hard time uncovering Wellness Tools for herself and thinks that working with Millie on it might help her. Millie is surprised to hear Sarah say that she, Millie, could be helpful. She has never thought of herself as helpful before, but rather as someone who needs help. She has also told Sarah that she is afraid that, this time, they will never let her leave the hospital. Millie says that she knows about WRAP but has a hard time even getting started on it and thinking of Wellness Tools in the hospital. Sarah and Millie begin to discuss Wellness Tools. Sarah says that making her bed every morning is a Wellness Tool for her—that when she makes the bed she feels better. She says it also makes it harder for her to crawl back into bed when she really wants to get up and keep going. Millie says she didn't think anything that simple could be a Wellness Tool. She suggests that maybe smiling at someone could be a Wellness Tool for her, or complimenting someone at dinner. As their discussions moved along, they each discovered Wellness Tools that neither would have thought of on their own.

Wellness Tools can include just about anything, and, through discussion and Peer Support, people can come up with things that neither person might have thought of on their own.

Over time people get used to using Wellness Tools and other activities to help them get through difficult times. As they begin to work on WRAP, the strategies they use may be different from those they would use later. It may not be useful to make major changes all at once, or ever, unless the person wants to. For instance, it may be unreasonable to expect a person to start Peer Support, begin therapy, quit smoking and get in the habit of eating three healthy meals a day, all at the same time. These changes usually happen gradually and people decide for themselves if they will make these changes, when they will make these changes and how they will make them. What they can do is support each other in ways that work and enhance the relationship, and to remind each other that everyone is capable of making positive changes (even when one of us is not so sure).

Over-eating is an example of a coping strategy (Wellness Tool) that a person uses to get through those times when the emotional pain is intense. As they work on their WRAP with another person, they may find that they are able to call each other on the phone and talk about the urge to over-eat without actually acting on it. Gradually they may notice that this changes as they use WRAP and Peer Support to help themselves feel better and to prevent more difficult times. They may find other Wellness Tools, like expressing emotions, going for a run, or doing some hard work, gradually reduce feelings of needing to over-eat. They may also find that they are spending more time with people who are supportive and staying away from people who treat them badly, and that they have made changes in their life, like getting their own living space, furthering their education, getting a job or doing volunteer work, that increases their overall sense of well being.

When we talk in our groups about things that are not generally considered "appropriate," like alcohol, illegal substance use, or self-injury, some people get uncomfortable and have a strong urge to be judgmental. In the past it has not been acceptable to say we feel like hurting ourselves, for fear we'd end up hospitalized or in seclusion and restraints, or at least sternly chastised, or to say that we were going to continue to drink, but do it less and less. The issue becomes more complex when people say they are going to use these strategies as Wellness Tools. For some of us, these are tools we've developed to survive very, very difficult situations. Although these activities are often judged negatively and severely, if we think about them relative to what has happened to us in our lives, they may make sense in some circumstances. As the experts on ourselves, we are the only ones who can make these decisions. Good facilitators and supportive peers recognize and encourage important conversations about these topics.

Here is a Role Play that illustrates a Wellness Tool that others might not approve of:

Samira: I have this Wellness Tool that I have been using for over 40 years but you might not think it is a Wellness Tool. Look at my arms. I have been cutting myself. Whenever the pain gets too bad I cut myself and then I feel better. It really works for me.

Grace: Wow, that's really brave of you to talk about.

Samira: I am shocked that you are calling it brave. Every time someone finds out about it, I get in all kinds of trouble. That is why I really wasn't sure I should share it with you.

Grace: I guess what I'm reacting to is that you did bring it up. A lot of people would have kept it hidden.

Samira: I know. Most people do and I didn't tell anyone for a long time. But then they notice it when I have testing at the hospital and I get this big lecture about how I need to stop doing that—that I should not cut myself. And it makes it all worse.

Grace: I can relate to that, when people used to tell me I had to stop I just felt so much shame.

Samira: It sounds like you have cut yourself. Is that what you are saying?

Grace: I used to and I know what you mean about making things better. The only trouble for me was that I'd feel better for a while and then I'd need to cut deeper...

Samira: Then it gets dangerous. I know that. I have been making sure I don't cut deeper. I think it is like drinking wine. I have made it a point never to drink more than ½ a glass of wine a day and that works for me and I enjoy it. I am careful about the cutting and I always keep in clean. Right now I don't want to do anything about it. Maybe someday I will but I am not sure. For me, right now, it is a Wellness Tool. Do I have to show this plan to someone else? Will I get in trouble for writing it? I am really glad I can be honest with you.

Grace: You don't have to show anyone the plan and you will not get in trouble with me for writing in it. I keep my own WRAP very private—I have a place that I hide it. I don't want anyone to see it that I don't want to see it. I think they would not understand. It sounds like cutting is really working for you right now. Are there times when it doesn't work so well?

Samira: I get concerned about it when it gets a little infected—afraid I have really hurt myself. And it doesn't help so much when I argue with my sister. But most of the time it works well.

Grace: Maybe you want to write the specifics of how you cut without getting an infection into your Wellness Toolbox as well as what you need to do when you argue with your sister.

Samira: Good idea. But I am still afraid someone will see my plan and I will get in trouble again. I have heard I can do it on line and it is confidential so I guess I will do that. It is hard to trust around these things. When I argue with my sister, it is best to just make an excuse and leave. Or if she is visiting me here, I tell a "white lie," that I have to go to a class or have an appointment with my doctor. I think I should be able to include telling white lies in my Toolbox. Sometime I may want to get on top of this cutting thing—stop doing it. When I am ready, can I talk to you about it?

Grace: Yes, you can definitely talk to me about it. You said something about getting in trouble again. Did you get in trouble for writing something in your WRAP plan in the past? Basically you can put anything in your Toolbox that works for you. What I'd like to be able to do is to raise questions that might help you think about things differently. And of course you can talk to me about any of this anytime. I'd be honored

Samira: I didn't get in trouble for putting something in my WRAP. But I did get in a lot of trouble for cutting. So I don't want that to happen again.

Grace: Yeah, I can understand that.

Peer Support Discussion Topics

What are some things that you do that help you feel the way you want to feel?

What do you do to help yourself feel better when you are not feeling well?

What are the things you need, or can do for each other, when you get into old patterns, like seeing yourself as sick?

How do you think you can discover new Wellness Tools?

Have you found any newsletters, magazines, websites or books that might be sources of Wellness Tools?

Would it ever be acceptable for people to talk about the need or desire to harm themselves (as a Wellness Tool) in order to relieve the pressure of keeping what happened to them secret, or to focus their attention away from emotional pain or "flashbacks"?

Would it be acceptable if people were working towards stopping a habit, but taking small steps, like having one less beer a day for a while and then reducing it more? Could they talk about having one beer a day, ongoing, without judgment from peers?

Have there been times in the past when talking about hard choices like hurting yourself has not been an option, or was even dangerous? Has that changed? If so, how? How do you feel about talking about hard choices?

Wellness Tools are the cornerstone of WRAP. For many people, uncovering Wellness Tools is a first step in understanding that we can help ourselves, that we have many simple, safe resources available to us that can move us forward in our lives. Figuring out our personal Wellness Tools can be facilitated by exploring ideas in depth in Peer Support, either when you are doing WRAP with another person or in a WRAP Group.

Chapter 10

The Daily Maintenance Plan

The next step in the WRAP process is developing a Daily Maintenance Plan. It includes three parts:

- What I'm like when I'm well.
- A list of things I need to do every day to stay well, called the Daily Maintenance Plan.
- A list of things I might need to do to stay well.

In a WRAP Group, a facilitator gives an overview of the three parts of this section. They would again describe each section as the group begins working on it. As with each section of WRAP, in WRAP Groups, responses to queries are recorded on easel pad paper for easy referral and possible inputting into a computer and making copies for each participant.

If you are working together one-on-one, you can discuss the section as you begin and then again, before you start working on each part. As with all sections of WRAP, allow plenty of time for in-depth dialogue using Peer Support.

The first part of this section is What I'm Like When I'm Well. The people that developed WRAP felt that, at the beginning of the plan, they needed to describe, possibly with a list of words, what they felt like when they were well. However, some people had problems with that idea. They said they couldn't remember ever feeling well. So it was decided that they could make a list of words that describe what they would like to feel like if they felt well. Whenever I think of that group of people working on developing what became WRAP, it reminds me of what a wonderful Peer Support process it was long before its value was recognized. This could also be a place where you include things you are working on or toward. Using Peer Support, this can be a process where something new and unexpected can come out of the conversation.

Sometimes we share things about ourselves that others have labeled "symptoms" or indicators that something is wrong with us, but it is "just the way we are," things like introverted, talkative, boisterous and argumentative. In addition to including this list in our WRAP so that we can refer to it from time to time, this exercise can also give validation, foster self-acceptance and acceptance of others, and normalize our experiences.

As I am working on this book, I realize that, in my own WRAP, this first part of the Daily Maintenance Plan is outdated. My perception of "What I am Like When I am Well" has changed dramatically over time. Through discussing it with peers, it has changed even more. When I first did this part of my WRAP, I did it on my own—not even with another person. Now that I understand that value of working on WRAP using Peer Support, I realize how limiting that was. Since then I have participated in many WRAP Groups, and while I have revised that first WRAP many, many times, I have neglected to change this part. Now as I am making many life changes, I am spending more time talking with several peers about this section so I can see things more clearly, possibly from angles I've not yet explored. My new description of myself when I am feeling well is:

I am more apt to be reasonable, to use good judgment and to be thoughtful and understanding in my relationships with others. I can let go of worries more easily. I am able to compartmentalize things I can't do anything about so they don't wear me down. I understand that I am a worthy person and have accomplished many amazing things in my life. I am content, calm, happy and self-confident.

Discussion Questions

What do I seem like to you when I am feeling well?

What indicators make you think that I am feeling well?

What do you feel like when you are feeling well?

Has anyone ever thought you were not feeling well when you really were feeling fine? What was that like for you? How did you handle it? How do you wish they had handled it?

Daily Maintenance Plan

Some of us have spent years of our lives in institutions, hospitals, prisons or in group homes, where we had little or no control over our lives. Some of us are still living in situations like that. Or we may be dissatisfied with other aspects of our lives or the way we feel. WRAP is a good place to start taking back control of our lives and moving towards the way we want to be and the way we want our lives to be—even when it seems like the journey might be long and arduous, and when we are not sure what is in store for us. The Daily Maintenance Plan is a good place to begin making the best of each and every day.

Again, the facilitators describe this section, or we talk about what it is with each other as we begin to work on this list. We can begin by talking about small things that we can do each day, Wellness Tools that we can use, to help assure that we will have a "good day" and "move forward," things like making our own bed, deciding what we want to eat, which groups we want to attend, going for a walk, spending time or more time talking to people we like, limiting things like cigarettes, coffee or sugar if they are issues, using or doing things in different ways, or challenging ourselves to try something new. Talking with others using Peer Support strategies can help us to figure this out. It doesn't have to happen in a formal group setting or at a special meeting, but it can.

A WRAP user said:

If I do the things on my Daily Maintenance Plan every day, I feel better. It supports what I am working toward in my life. When I neglect these things, I notice that it affects the way I feel. I have kept my list short enough so that on most days I can do everything on the list. I have a personal rule that I will not "give myself a hard time" if I don't do everything on the list.

In Peer Support, people may say that they have feelings and experiences that are so intrusive that developing a Daily Maintenance Plan seems impossible. If a person is constantly hearing voices, has extreme anxiety and fear, or is having a hard time staying still, it may be difficult to think of things to include on this list. The list can be very short. A list might be one thing—I will smile at one person each day or I will look one person in the eye. It may even be as simple as I'll brush my teeth, eat a piece of fruit or walk around the building outside. Having peers to talk to as we are developing these lists, and making these changes in our lives, affirms and supports us in this life changing process.

One woman in a Peer Support session said that she was in a short term hospital when she first learned about WRAP in a WRAP Group. She said the only thing she could think of to put on her list at that hard time was to brush her hair. So every day she brushed her hair (for her, brushing her hair is a Wellness Tool) and that was a beginning for her. Now she is long-term WRAP user and her list of things to do every day is longer—but not so long that she can't easily accomplish everything on it. As it becomes easier to accomplish the things on the Daily Maintenance Plan, more Wellness Tools can be put on the list, giving people more and more control over their life, making their life the way they want it to be.

Some of the things that have been on my Daily Maintenance Plan over time, things I uncovered in WRAP Groups, include—taking a shower, making my bed, drinking 6 glasses of water a day, eating 3 meals a day even if they are small (not skipping meals), taking my supplements, especially those that help me sleep, going to bed before 11, exercise for at least one half hour, connect with a person outside of my family, and do something creative for half an hour. I have been following this plan for a long time and have noticed that from time to time I have to add in particular things if my circumstances change—like recovering from a medical procedure or moving. I will talk to my peers about these changes as I make them.

Discussion Topics

Discuss times in our lives when we felt really good, what that felt like and what we might have done to make that happen.

Share words we might include on the list that describes us when we feel well.

What do you think about the idea of a Daily Maintenance Plan?

How has the Daily Maintenance Plan been helpful to people who have used it?

How do you balance what you need to do to take care of yourself every day and what you have to do (things that are your responsibility)?

Things I Might Need to Do

The next part of this section of the Daily Maintenance Plan is a list of things we don't always need to do, but that we might need or want to do sometimes. Some of these things, like paying bills, will create extra stress in our lives if we don't do them. As with each preceding section, we work together, discussing the section and sharing ideas using the Peer Support strategies, recording the group's ideas, sharing ideas with each other and writing down those ideas that resonate with us in our own plans. Some ideas that people often think of for this list include:

- spend time with a good friend or a peer supporter
- spend extra time with my partner
- be in touch with my family
- spend time with children or pets
- buy groceries
- pay bills
- get more sleep
- plan something fun for the weekend
- go for a long walk
- go to a support group

I have been talking with several peers about the things that cause stress in my life. Through these conversations, I have realized that taking care of the things I need to take care of on particular days is important to me, and that I find myself getting very discouraged when I don't do something I had committed to or that puts me "behind." I don't necessarily need to do them every day, but I know if I need to do them and I don't, I will feel stressed—and that stress can sometimes keep me from moving forward in my life, doing the things I want to do and being the way I want to be.

My own list turned out to be a list of questions:

Do I need to check in with any family members, specific friends or supporters?

Is there anything that has to do with my work that needs immediate attention?

Is there anything that has to do with my volunteer work that I need to take care of?

Is there anything about my health that needs attention?

Do I need to take extra time to relax today?

Do I need to spend more time today doing things I love to do?

Do I need to reach out for extra Peer Support?

Elsa and Tara were discussing this section of the plan. Elsa said that she didn't really understand this section of WRAP. Tara said that she thought it was a way to keep yourself on track, doing the things you need to do to avoid stress. She said that she feels better when she checks in with her grandchildren most days. But she doesn't need to do it every day. And she knows she doesn't need to vacuum and dust every day but from time to time it helps her to feel better. She asked Elsa what she felt she might need to do. Elsa shared that she is thinking of going back to work and that she would benefit from working on that issue some days but not every day. Tara told her that when she was thinking of going back to work a vocational counselor was helpful to her. Elsa asked more about it and decided this would be something she will pursue. She thought that making appointments and contacts related to getting a job, like with a vocational counselor, would be good additions to her list of things she needs to do from time to time.

In this example, the discussion using Peer Support led to clarification of the topic and many different ideas for the list.

Discussion Questions

What do I need to do sometimes to keep my life manageable?

How do I feel when I don't do things when they need to be done, or when I would benefit from doing them?

Have you had times when you were avoiding doing things that you needed and wanted to do? If so, how did that make you feel? How did it affect you?

How do you think this list might be useful to you?

Chapter 11

Triggers

Now that we have completed the Wellness Toolbox and the Daily Maintenance Plan, we can continue to use what we have learned to think about and identify the times when we need to figure out what we need to do in specific situations. We will use the same process to do this that we used in developing the Daily Maintenance Plan—working our way through the next three sections of WRAP—Triggers, Early Warning Signs and When Things are Breaking Down, describing and discussing each section, uncovering ideas and tools from each other as we proceed, things we might not have thought of if working alone. Each of these sections includes a listing of signs or indicators we might experience or have experienced in the past, and responses or actions, Wellness Tools, we could use in these situations to move us toward what we want to do or the way we want to be.

As with the other sections of WRAP, WRAP Group facilitators describe each section of the plan as the group begins to work on it, then lead the group through developing an understanding of the section and developing lists of indicators and responses that are recorded on an easel pad and input on a computer so that copies can easily be made for each participant. PowerPoint slides from the *WRAP Facilitators Manual* and examples from the facilitators increase understanding. In working together one on one or with several people, you can come up with ideas that will strengthen this part of the plan.

Triggers

In the past, when I thought of myself as being mentally ill, if something bad happened that was upsetting, I either got more and more upset, went into a panic, got confused, lashed out at someone or something, or did something that worsened the situation. Sometimes I didn't even know what the "Trigger" was, what had upset me. The situation sometimes escalated to the point that someone would suggest I needed more medication, tried to control me in some way, or ostracized me. As things progressed, I felt worse and worse. The end result could be what I then referred to as a "crisis," which I thought, and others confirmed for me, was a result of my "mental illness." People would say, "It is just because you are mentally ill, dear," instead of saying this is a normal reaction to something like having your purse stolen, hearing that a friend has been in a bad accident, being teased and bullied by someone you had trusted, or the anniversary date of a terrible loss.

Now I have completed the Triggers section of my WRAP. I did it with the support of a peer. I wish I could have done it in a WRAP Group but that wasn't possible at this time. While I could never name all my potential Triggers, I now realize what many of them are and if one comes up that I may not have previously named, I recognize it for what it is. Using my Wellness Toolbox, I have developed a list of Wellness Tools I can use to get through difficult times. I have choices of tools I can use in various situations. I don't need to resort to behaviors that I used when I believed I was "mentally ill." Now I see myself as a normal person who has normal responses to difficult and upsetting times, and have a plan of Wellness Tools to use if they come up to avoid further repercussion. Having this plan itself helps me feel more comfortable, to be able to be with my discomfort, or even resolve the situation, and encourage interaction and support from others.

For some people, the word "Trigger" means things are out of control and there is nothing they can do about it; an anticipated or unanticipated event. Sometimes people accuse others of triggering us—"you're triggering me"—when what's really happening is that something they are doing is causing me to feel uncomfortable. We can think of Wellness Tools we can use to handle situations like that. For instance, suppose that Jack is telling the group about an incident with his brother that involved physical abuse. Doria noticed that she was feeling more and more anxious and upset. In the past she might have called out, "Stop. You are triggering me." Instead she took responsibility for the way she was feeling, used some Wellness Tools—leaving the situation, taking a short walk and listening to music on her iPhone, and doing some deep breathing. When she returned to the group, they had moved on to a different topic. Later she shared her experience with the group, telling them that hearing about the abuse was hard for her so she decided to take a break and come back to the group later. She said in the past she might have blurted out something that would have been uncomfortable and embarrassing.

I have developed a list of Triggers through years of going to WRAP Groups and Peer Support. However, as part of living, I often discover new ones, most often through Peer Support. Through the WRAP process and with the Triggers Action Plan I recognize Triggers and respond in ways that honor and support me and others as I move forward.

- anniversary dates of losses or trauma
- traumatic news events
- being overly tired
- family friction
- spending too much time alone
- being judged, criticized, teased or put down
- financial problems
- physical illness
- sexual harassment
- feeling unsafe
- feeling left out
- things that remind me of times when I was abandoned
- people trying to get close to me before I am comfortable with them
- excessive stress
- guilt
- substance abuse
- feeling shamed
- blaming myself

For example, a woman was in a restaurant having lunch with a group of friends. One of the friends made a comment that was very embarrassing to her. She yelled at the other woman, threw a glass of water in her face and stormed out of the restaurant. Afterward she felt embarrassed and humiliated by her own actions. She also noticed that friends stopped including her in invitations. In considering this event and discussing it with her peers, she realized there were other ways she could have handled the situation. She could have told the woman that she was embarrassed and asked her not to do it again. She could have asked the woman to go outside with her to discuss the situation. She could have asked another friend to go outside and talk with her to do a "reality check" and figure out how to handle it. She could have taken a "time out" and gone to the rest room to think about it. She could have ignored it until later and spoken with the women who embarrassed her afterward. There were lots of options that she explored in discussing this experience with her peers. When we get together to work on WRAP, we may want to share some situations we have experienced and discuss possible solutions—new ways of responding to troubling situations.

Some Triggers are "too huge" to predict in advance—and we don't want to stay focused on the possibility that they might happen, things like catastrophic illness, accidents, fires, storms, and loss of any kind. Life wouldn't be much fun if we spent a lot of time focusing on those kinds of things. Through several extended Peer Support discussions, it was decided that if any of these horrible things happened, even several at once, we could use our Triggers responses much more intensively and refer back to our list of Wellness Tools for more ideas. Peer Support would support us in that process. And, depending on the situation, our circle of Peer Supporters might become very big.

I was on a plane flying from Chicago to Hartford many years ago. After we had only been in the air long enough for lunch to be served, the cabin filled with smoke—a "triggering" event in itself. There were about 25 people on the plane. The steward immediately removed the lunch trays and the pilot announced an emergency landing. As the plane banked sharply and headed into Detroit, the passengers and the crew became Peer Supporters—there for each other, holding hands and watching in horror as the airport got close too quickly and we watched the fire trucks racing across the tarmac. We landed safely and they evacuated us quickly to a small private room. In that room it was like we had known each other forever—sharing our thoughts and feelings as we had felt the end was near and our elation that we had been given another chance. One interesting thing we discovered, each of us had saved our bag of M&Ms from the lunch trays (a Wellness Tool?) as they were being hastily taken away. Peer Support, in even this most dire situation, was there for us.

Through ongoing practice and Peer Support, I have discovered Wellness Tools that often work for me when a "triggering" event occurs. I have listed them in my Triggers Action Plan. My list is too long to include all of it here. You can't use these Wellness Tools all at once, or predict in advance when a triggering event might occur, so include many options, many Wellness Tools.

If necessary, I can refer to my long list of Wellness Tools for additional things I can do in specific situations.

- Avoiding reading the newspaper and watching the news on television
- Avoiding certain people
- Doing something I really enjoy, like watching a movie or working on a quilt
- Playing the piano
- Doing one or several deep breathing or meditation exercises
- Talking with a peer
- Crying
- Taking a nap
- Reading a novel (I am always in the midst of one)
- Extra time with grandchildren
- Calling a family member
- Taking a long walk
- Taking a time out
- Eating cookies or ice cream
- Follow one of my "daily plans" for difficult days

A friend's husband died very unexpectedly. It was horrible and she experienced the worst of difficult times for many, many months. She barely survived. This was long before we were talking about WRAP and Peer Support. But in looking back to that time, that is what happened. A group of committed people, peers, gathered around her. We got together with her as a group as often as possible. Sometimes it was only a couple of us. Sometimes it was all of us. Sometimes it was just one of us. We talked about what we were working on, not just for my friend, but for all of us as individuals and as a group, learning together how to move forward—it was mutual. We kept this level of support going for many, many months. My friend was "dreading" the first anniversary of her husband's death. We came up with something that we thought would work for any of us, the concept of a daily plan (now a Wellness Tool). We would plan the anniversary or "triggering" day well in advance. It included having someone in the group spending the night at her house the night before and the night after the anniversary day. They would go to a favorite restaurant for breakfast, followed by a long hike (one of her favorite activities), then lunch with a group of friends, a trip in the afternoon with a friend to a museum in a nearby town, with a special restaurant for dinner, followed by a movie. This was her plan. Through all of this, others of us thought about her situation and our own unique situations and the things that might happen in our own lives. The way it evolved was truly remarkable.

Peer Support Discussion Topics

Discuss times when triggering events occurred, how people responded to them, how it felt for them and how it worked in their lives.

Share ideas for working through the hardest of times.

Discuss Wellness Tools that can be used in unexpected situations where options are limited.

Chapter 12

Early Warning Signs

The next section is Early Warning Signs. Early Warning Signs are subtle signs that things are not quite right. Sometime we don't notice them, or if we do notice them, we ignore them. We may be unclear about why we feel the way we do, but we notice that we feel differently than we usually feel, and perhaps uncomfortable or uneasy. Many people have reported that developing an awareness of these signs by using WRAP and Peer Support, and responding to these signs right away, with specific Wellness Tools, helps them do what they need to do to move toward feeling the way they want to feel and doing the things they want to do.

In a WRAP Group, the facilitators begin working on this section by describing what Early Warning Signs are. Participants then share their own Early Warning Signs, with responses being recorded on an easel pad. The facilitators encourage conversation that may lead to a deeper awareness of Early Warning Signs or that help participants discover Early Warning Signs they may not have thought of. If people are working together one-on-one on WRAP, they begin by discussing what Early Warning Signs are, then share their own, discussing each sign as they do so.

I used to ignore Early Warning Signs. I just kept "pushing through" and hoping they would go away. Usually the opposite happened. I felt worse and worse and worse. Over the years I have had many discussions about Early Warning Signs in WRAP Groups and times when I have been talking about my WRAP with a peer. As I have done that, I have become more and more aware of my Early Warning Signs.

Some examples of Early Warning Signs that others have come up with in WRAP Groups or in working with a peer include:

- anxiety or nervousness
- forgetfulness

- lack of motivation
- feeling slowed down or speeded up
- avoiding doing things on Daily Maintenance Plan
- avoiding others or isolating
- beginning of irrational thought patterns
- increased irritability or negativity
- increase in smoking
- not keeping appointments
- spending money impulsively
- feelings of discouragement or hopelessness
- increase in drinking alcohol
- failing to buckle my seat belt
- not answering the phone
- overeating or under-eating
- obsessively counting everything
- noticing that everything seems overwhelming
- not sleeping
- waking at 3 am and not being able to go back to sleep
- not being able to fall asleep
- thinking a lot about death and dying
- crying all the time
- being fearful without knowing why
- being fearful of everything

Joyce, Bill, Tammy and Loretta have been meeting every week to work on their WRAPs. Loretta found the concept of Early Warning Signs difficult to understand until she heard examples of these signs from her peers. Tammy and Bill described the process they went through to discover their Early Warning Signs, sharing ideas and then expanding on these ideas through conversation. Joyce said that she had been working on the Early Warning Signs section on her own, but that it was hard for her. The group meetings were working better for her.

Role Play

A person is trying to understand what Early Warning Signs are and the other person is trying to clarify that for her.

Discussion Topics

What happened just before you noticed the Early Warning Sign?

Do you have any Early Warning Signs that you think might be unique to you?

Early Warning Signs Action Plan

After identifying Early Warning Signs, the facilitators describe the Early Warning Signs Action Plan, sharing some of their own experiences. Or if you are working with another person, you discuss what the Action Plan is. This Action Plan is different from the Triggers Action Plan. The Triggers Action Plan gives a list of options. While this plan can contain options, most people choose to develop something more like a daily plan to use when they notice Early Warning Signs. If I can, I like to take the day or several days off and follow a specific daily plan that I have developed that tells me what to do each hour of the day. I include choices and I know that I can always refer to my Wellness Toolbox or to my peers for more ideas. We can figure out our personal plan by discussing it with peers. In a WRAP Group the facilitators describe the Action Plan, perhaps using PowerPoint Slides, and then people in the group discuss the Action Plan and share ideas for what they would include in their plan. If we are developing this section of WRAP with another person, we talk together about the plan as we develop it.

I used to think of Early Warning Signs as something that were out of my control. I would worry about things that others might see as "normal" difficult feelings. Because I've worked hard to identify these signs with the help of numerous peers, I can make choices about what I want to do about them when I notice them. Now I'm not afraid of my own feelings and, more importantly, others aren't afraid for me.

Now when I notice Early Warning Signs, I follow my plan. And when I do, the Early Warning Signs usually go away and I get on with doing what I want to be doing. Sometimes it's hard to take action, but I have learned that my best strategy is to be OK with my discomfort and to persist in "working towards."

Discussing Early Warning Signs Action Plans with peers can increase the awareness of Wellness Tools that can be used for addressing these signs.

My own plan is as follows:

Each day until I don't notice these Early Warning Signs I will:

Do the things on my Daily Maintenance Plan whether I feel like it or not.

Have at least 15 minutes with a peer supporter or attend a WRAP support group.

Do three relaxation exercises that are at least 10 minutes long.

In addition I might choose to:

- Write in my journal for at least 15 minutes each day.
- Spend at least 1 hour involved in an activity I enjoy.
- Ask others to take over my household responsibilities for a day.
- Go to a support group meeting.
- Understand that I will be uncomfortable for a while.
- Do a favorite visualization exercise.
- Spend extra time drawing or working on a creative project.

Each part of WRAP is a bit more challenging than the last. Using what we have learned in developing the previous sections and continuing to add to our Wellness Toolbox, supports the process of developing a WRAP.

The next section of WRAP is "When Things Are Breaking Down."

Chapter 13

When Things Are Breaking Down: Avoiding a Crisis

"When Things are Breaking Down" is another way of saying "when things have gotten much worse." Many people, including myself, have used this section intensively to "Avoid a Crisis" and all of the possible related traumas and repercussions of a Crisis. I have been successful in using this section to avoid a Crisis since the development of WRAP in 1997. Using Peer Support, both in groups and with a peer supporter, I have uncovered new tools and strategies that work better and better for me in difficult times. I include them in my ongoing revisions of this section of my plan.

If you have reached this point in your WRAP, you may feel really awful; or perhaps you feel wonderful, but your peers are telling you that your behavior is unusual or troubling. This is an important time. You can make a decision to do something about it. You can decide that you want to Avoid a Crisis **and that it may be hard**. Or you can just allow the troubling feelings and behaviors to take control. The choice is up to you.

You may want to begin working on this section by discussing, with your peers, times When Things Were Breaking Down in the past, and looking at what happened just before you felt that way. You might remember that you lost your job, had a hassle about benefits or had a troubling visit with family members. Perhaps you were very overtired or had been eating a lot of junk food. This can help in identifying the signs that Things are Breaking Down and in choosing actions you can take to move through this time and back to feeling the way you want to feel and doing the things you want to do.

When Things are Breaking Down and you want to Avoid a Crisis, the signs are usually obvious to others, or at least you are aware of them yourself. You may still try to ignore them, hope that they will go away or worry that they won't. I used to ignore them, but these days, with all my WRAP experience, I don't do that. I have a strong commitment to myself, my family and my supporters that I will take the actions I need to take to Avoid a Crisis.

The signs might include things like:

- Feeling very oversensitive and fragile
- Irrational responses to events and the actions of others
- Feeling very needy, like you want someone to take care of you
- Unable to sleep for ____ (how long?)
- Sleeping all the time
- Avoiding eating
- Wanting to be totally alone
- Avoiding peers and other people you care about
- Racing thoughts
- Risk taking behaviors, like driving too fast
- Thoughts of self-harm
- Being obsessed with negative thoughts
- Inability to slow down
- Bizarre behaviors (describe them)
- Disassociation (blacking out, spacing out, losing time)
- Seeing things that aren't there
- Taking out anger on others
- Chain smoking
- Spending excessive amounts of money (Say how much that means for you.)
- Food abuse
- NOT feeling
- Suicidal thoughts
- Paranoia (thinking others are "out to get you")

In the past, you might have called a crisis line, asked for additional medications or to been admitted to a hospital when you had these feelings or behaviors. That is often not necessary and may not be in your best interest. It is too easy to get into all kinds of difficulties at these times, especially if you are interacting with people who don't know you and who think your behavior is dangerous. You could easily end up in restraints or seclusion or in some other awful situation. Instead, you can use your Wellness Tools and the Action Plan you have developed for dealing with difficult times, times "When Things Are Breaking Down: Avoiding a Crisis," to manage the situation yourself.

After identifying feelings and behaviors that indicate Things Are Breaking Down and you want to Avoid a Crisis, working with peers, you can develop an Action Plan. The Action Plan now needs to be very directive, with fewer choices and clear instructions. Report your successes and failures, and refine your Action Plan each time you use it to improve its effectiveness.

You may get some ideas for the When Things Are Breaking Down/Avoiding a Crisis Action Plan from the following list and from your peers as you do this work together:

- Talk to peer supporters.
- Arrange for someone to stay with me around the clock until I feel better.
- Make sure I am doing everything on my Daily Maintenance Plan.
- Arrange for at least three days off from any responsibilities.
- Have at least two peer counseling sessions daily.
- Do three deep breathing relaxation exercises daily.
- Write in my journal for half an hour.
- Spend at least one hour exercising.
- Spend at least two hours doing something I really enjoy.
- Connect with peers online.

Following are some responses from peers to a Facebook post asking them about their When Things Are Breaking Down Action Plans:

Amy says, "I have great friends, and we seem to support each other in the good and the bad times. Hospitals are not really my thing any more. Getting through life is more important to me. My cat is very important to me also. I make "to do" lists and try to accomplish them, and when I do something on the list it feels good to cross it off. Sometimes they are simply lists and others are more complex. Completing these lists makes me feel like I have run a marathon. I have also learned that my supporters are not going to do the hard work for me. I have to do it myself. They are there to help me and support me and to listen to me. We have an understanding and an open relationship. I now can ask for what I need, not what I want. It has taken me a long, long, long time to learn this."

Susan says, "I avoid negativity. Each morning when my alarm cat wakes me up, I look out my window and smile…today is another great day for adventure!"

Robin says, "I ask others to just listen, not judge...I think it's easy to believe no one understands, but in some ways, in their own way, they do. Most importantly, I take time for myself, if it's under the covers, calling a friend, taking a walk or taking a few days away to collect myself."

Sherri says, "I get really hyper and irritable. I take things personally and want to isolate. I lose interest in food and can't sleep. Those are signs that I am headed for a bad place if I don't take care of myself. I do self-care. I reach out to people who love me. I make myself go out. I eat little bits to keep up strength."

One thing you can discuss with peers about this time is discomfort. You may have been led to believe that it is not OK to feel uncomfortable. You were taught that if you don't feel fine, you need to take a pill, reach out to a health care provider, or perhaps be admitted to a health care facility or hospital for treatment. In developing plans, we may want to think about just being with our discomfort, examining it, responding to it in some way, like crying, fussing, whining (to ourselves or a willing listener) or ignoring it. If we wait it out, it may just go away. We could discuss with our peers the times when we stayed with our discomfort and what happened when we did that. Perhaps we can use "staying with our discomfort" as a Wellness Tool and include it in our Action Plans.

Consider the following role play that may increase your understanding of using Peer Support for the When Things Are Breaking Down section of the Wellness Recovery Action Plan.

Ellen: If I'm not sleeping I feel really agitated. Yeah. I have been like this lots of times before and going to the hospital and getting meds is usually the best thing for me…But I hate it. And sometimes they put me in restraints because they think I am going to hurt myself.

Sherm: That sounds terrible, what kinds of things have been happening when you're not sleeping and you've felt really agitated?

Ellen: Well, just about everything. One time my partner had just broken up with me. I think she was seeing somebody else. And she was really mean and rude to me. And then they reduced my benefits so I thought I might have to move.

Sherm: Wow, that's a lot of stuff.

Ellen: It's too much for me. That is when I think I need a break and that the hospital would be a good thing. Another time I stole something and got caught on purpose so I could spend a few days in jail. Sometimes I just need to get away from everything. Things get so bad.

Sherm: I can relate to wanting to get away from everything. I actually used to end up going to the hospital when I felt like that as well. But I am curious about why it works for you?

Ellen: That's a good question. Well, there is food and I like to eat. It is comforting to me. And it feels safe there. And there are people to talk to.

Sherm: Yes, many of the same reasons I went to the hospital until I realized that being comfortable wasn't the same as being safe.

Ellen: What do you mean that being comfortable wasn't the same as being safe?

Sherm: I guess I think of comfort now as feeling calm and safety I think of as more like, "I can take a risk." Like I trust myself and those around me to help me to "spread my wings…" Does that make sense?

Ellen: If I were safe, I wouldn't have to be afraid that somebody was going to treat me badly. I have not been safe very much in my life. Have you ever felt safe?

Sherm: Yes, I think so, but it's changed over time. I used to think safety had to do with other people making decisions for me, but now I think safety really is about having choices. Real choices

Ellen: Having choices. That is a different way to look at it. Right now I don't feel like I have many choices. But maybe I do. Can you make real choices for yourself now?

Sherm: Sometimes it's hard and I make bad choices but at least they're my choices.

Ellen: I guess there are a few choices I could make. Maybe one would be staying away from people who treat me badly. If I tried that one, maybe I could figure out a few more.

Sherm: Sounds like a really good idea. Do you know when people are going to treat you badly? I'm always surprised by that one, because I just don't expect it.

Ellen: Well there are certain people that I have learned will treat me well at first and then turn on me. I could stay away from them. And then stay away from places where the rude people hang out. Like there is this place in our town where it seems everyone goes to hang out. And I go there sometimes. And the people are not very nice to each other. I need to think of someplace else to go.

Sherm: That sounds like a very good start!

Ellen: Are these things—making choices and staying away from certain people and places—part of WRAP?

Sherm: They certainly can be part of your Wellness Toolbox.

Ellen: And the kinds of Tools I would use When Things Are Breaking Down for me. Let's work on this some more another time.

Sherm: Sounds good.

Discussion Topics

What are some signs for you that Things are Breaking Down?

Why would you want to Avoid a Crisis?

How have you known When Things Were Breaking Down or getting much worse?

How have you dealt with situations like these in the past? Do you think there are other ways you might deal with them? What are they?

How do you feel about being with discomfort? Do you think that might be a Wellness Tool for you? Can you think of other unusual Wellness Tools that might work to help you move out of this difficult space and move forward in your life?

Describe times in your life When Things Were Breaking Down and you were trying to Avoid a Crisis. How did you handle them? How did that work for you? If you would like to do it differently another time, what would that be like?

Completing the Wellness Toolbox and the first four sections of WRAP is a major achievement. By this time you may be seeing yourself in new ways and feeling that you have power and control over your own life and that you can do what you need to do to get well, to stay well and even to Avoid a Crisis. You are more familiar with using Peer Support with WRAP and you can see how effective it is in helping you to move forward in your life.

Veronica says, "Since I've been to WRAP Groups and trained to facilitate them, I never go into Crisis. I have the Tools inside me and they seem to work automatically as life events happen."

Chapter 14

Crisis Plan (Advance Directive)

In this chapter you will be working, section by section, through the process of developing a Crisis Plan (Advance Directive) using Peer Support.

A Crisis Plan is the same as, or similar to, an Advance Directive. It is designed to tell others what to do when we can't take care of ourselves. Mental health and other kinds of health care systems are mandating that every person who uses their services have a Crisis Plan or Advance Directive in their file. People can choose to use their WRAP Advance Directive in this way. As with the rest of WRAP, people develop these plans for themselves with the collaborators and peers of their choice, if and when they feel ready to do so. **The Plan can be kept in an agency file if, and only if, the person who developed it wants it to be there.** People can give copies of these plans to their supporters and to the health care organizations and other agencies of their choice. These would be the people who assist and support them when the plan indicates they should do so.

Discussion Topics

Who do I want to have copies of my Advance Directive/Crisis Plan?

Do I want my Plan included in my file at a health care agency? Why or why not? Are there any agencies or organizations that I want to have copies of my Crisis Plan?

Who do I want to collaborate with on developing my plan?

What is "Crisis"?

Mary Ellen: How would you describe a crisis?

Shery: I'm not sure. I guess it has something to do with being overwhelmed beyond what your normal resources can handle.

Mary Ellen: How would you relate to a person who is in that situation?

Shery: I think I would try to get a feel for where they were at, what they were feeling, thinking about, etc.

Crisis has different meanings for different people. The following statements were responses to a Facebook post asking people to share what crisis is to them.

Astrid says, "A crisis to me is wanting to knock myself out with the drug I was addicted to."

Maureen says, "For me a crisis is when all the joy and hope have been sucked right out of my life. I feel nothing. I tend to isolate from everyone—my family, friends, etc. I lose interest in even the simplest things, like going for walks, listening to music and reading (I am an avid reader)."

Joy says, "To me a crisis is when I cannot get out. I begin to loose all contact with reality and need to get away. My voices tell me I'm no good. I begin to deteriorate by not bathing or changing my clothes. I begin to believe that I'm the Virgin Mary and need to find my son, or others are after me because they have programmed a device into my head. I begin to scare my family and friends."

Glyn writes, "I celebrate crisis as an opportunity for change and growth. Crisis to me means things are not working in my life and when I won't listen, my body and my mind make me listen by shutting down until I have to stop. I come to a crossroads in my life where I have a choice about which way I go—to carry on the negative path I'm on or do what my WRAP tells me in Wellness Tools and Daily Maintenance Plan. WRAP is simple, but as a human being, I make it hard."

When I began doing this work, it was assumed that everyone who had mental health difficulties would have times of crisis, that it was part of the "disability," that there was nothing we could do to prevent crisis after crisis, and that at these times we would not recognize what was going on. Others would have to step in and do things to make us do what they felt was right for us. They may have called a Crisis Team and we may have been put in handcuffs and taken to a jail or a locked mental health facility. Other things may have been done to us that were not helpful, were harmful and that further traumatized us. These things can and do still happen to people. Now many of us avoid this situation almost all the time by using WRAP and Peer Support and having supporters who walk with us and understand what we need through the hardest of times.

My own description of what a crisis is for me has changed over the years as I have become more aware of the many things I can do to help myself in what used to be the hardest of times—times when I felt like there was nothing I could do to help myself. Many of the signs of crisis that I included in my early Crisis Plans are now in my When Things are Breaking Down section. With WRAP, people report that they no longer, or only occasionally, have a crisis where others need to "take care of" or "help" them. Now they know the Wellness Tools they need to use to get through these times.

Discussion Topics

What does crisis mean to you in your life?

Has your definition of crisis changed over time? If so, how?

If we develop Crisis Plans ourselves, with our peers, and if the plan is followed, it keeps us in control, even when it may feel like things are out of control. Others will be doing things with us and for us that support us in moving out of this situation, rather than things they think might be helpful or should be done. In the past, when things were done to us that others thought would be helpful or that were for the convenience of other people or an institution, we generally felt worse—sometimes much worse. Having our own Crisis Plan can help prevent the trauma of coercion, restraint, isolation and forced medication.

Many people find that developing the Crisis Plan or Advance Directive is the most difficult part of developing a Wellness Recovery Action Plan, and that it may take more time to develop than all of the other sections of WRAP combined. People also find that, having already worked on their Wellness Toolbox and the other parts of WRAP, they are more prepared to work on this document.

People find that when they develop the Crisis Plan with peers or in a WRAP Group, they are able to uncover options they might not have considered on their own, and have opportunities to discuss them so that they can develop a plan that is most effective.

Your Advance Directives/Crisis Plans need to be clear about what you do want and what you don't want to have happen to you. This helps you to avoid having things done to you that you do not want done or that are hurtful or traumatizing. The involvement of peers in the process, particularly peers who may be supporting and advocating for you in a crisis, increases the likelihood that your intentions are easily understood and that the plan will be followed.

While other parts of WRAP are only for use by the person who is developing the Wellness Recovery Action Plan, the Crisis Plan is given to others when it is completed so they will know how to support you when needed. This is a different focus than the other parts of WRAP. The first four sections of WRAP only need to be understood by the person who is developing their WRAP. The Crisis Plan, to be effective, needs to be written so others can **easily understand** what you mean. **It is up to you to decide who you want to give it to, who you want to support you and who you don't want involved.**

Discussion Topics

What do you see as the benefits of developing your Crisis Plan/Advance Directive with peers who are also working on their plan?

Do you think it is important to have a Crisis Plan/Advance Directive? If so, why? If not, why not?

Do you agree that a Crisis Plan/Advance Directive needs to be clear and tell others exactly what to do? If so, why? If not, why not?

Why do you need to give copies of your Crisis Plan to your supporters? How do you feel about that?

There is a form for the Crisis Plan or Advance Directive in the Appendix. Many of the resources listed at www.WRAPandRecoveryBooks.com include Crisis Plan forms. It is also on the WRAP app and part of the Build Your Own WRAP online program

Part 1. What I am Like When I am Well

The first section of the Crisis Plan is the same as Part One of the Daily Maintenance section of WRAP—**What I Am Like When I Am Well**. This is included in case someone you have never met at an agency, care facility or some sort of emergency service is trying to follow your plan. It is to keep them from making invalid assumptions, assuming some of your behaviors or ways of being are "symptoms of illness" rather than how you usually are.

For instance, you might be a very quiet person, or one who considers carefully what you are going to say before speaking. Someone might assume it is because you are "depressed." A person who talks a lot might be accused of being "manic" or "bipolar." If you commonly have things like spasms on the side of your face, a strong limp, or tremor, someone might try to treat it when it is not a sign of a crisis and it does not need treatment at all. You can copy the section "What I'm Like When I'm Well" from the beginning of WRAP and insert it in the Crisis Plan here, or, you can develop one more specifically for the Crisis Plan.

This section can be written in list form, sentences or even several paragraphs that you feel reflect who you are. If you use the WRAP app, you could have a recording on your phone where you describe yourself when you are feeling well, along with a picture or video of yourself.

Discussion Topics

What are you like when you feel well?

What are signs that might be taken as "symptoms" by someone who doesn't know you?

Behaviors or Signs

The next section of the Crisis Plan or Advance Directive is a listing of behaviors or signs that others might notice that would let them know when you need assistance and support. This needs to be carefully considered. Most people don't want others to step in and take over when you can, and want to, take care of things yourself. Yet this is a common occurrence. Others think they need to "help us" rather than support and "learn" with us as we work our way through difficult times. This section attempts to keep that from happening. The key question is "When do I **really** need someone else to take over responsibility for my care?" Many people get clarity on this issue thorough discussing it with others, through Peer Support.

I have been working so intensively with WRAP in my life and sharing it with others, that my list of signs that I need someone to take over is much different than it used to be. Almost every sign that I used to have in my Crisis Plan is now is in the When Things are Breaking Down: Avoiding a Crisis section of my WRAP. Because I use the rest of my WRAP intensively, I never get to that place, a place I used to call a "crisis," where I thought things were happening **to** me. Instead I learn from the situation and move towards doing things differently.

While my previous Crisis Plan used to list signs like crying all the time, not eating for three days and seeing thing that aren't there, now my signs of Crisis list would say:

Unconscious
Not responding at all to stimuli
Not having moved in over 4 hours
Unable to move at all
Physically hurting others
Taking direct and specific action to end my life

Discussing this part of the plan with peers can bring up confusing and embarrassing feelings about difficult times in the past. People may want to talk through some of those times with a view toward learning from them and figuring out what they would do now instead. Or they may choose not to revisit past history and want to start from a new and different place.

Sometimes people feel uncomfortable or embarrassed about sharing when working on this part of the plan. They may want to be with that discomfort, sharing or not, as always, their choice. Learning together can help ease that discomfort and uncover thoughts and ideas that will make this part of the plan more effective. People may choose to discuss difficult times they have had, and times when they wish others had responded differently. This discussion often leads people to rethink their definition of a crisis or what a crisis really is for them.

I used to think I was in a crisis when I was feeling very agitated and anxious, and when I was crying a lot. Then I realized, there are lots of things I can do to help myself at that time, and it isn't really a crisis at all. I can call a peer or a good friend. I can do some of my relaxation techniques. I can take a long walk. *I can sit with my discomfort.* I can express my emotions in a way that feels right to me—having a long crying spell, laughing a lot, shouting, etc. I began to think that the only time I am really in a crisis and need others to take over for me is if I am comatose, or so lethargic I literally can't move to feed myself, or if I am hurting myself (life-threatening) or threatening to hurt others. Everything that used to be on my old list, things like pacing, counting things over and over and not getting out of bed, are things I can manage in the "When Things are Breaking Down: Avoiding a Crisis" section, using my Action Plan and Peer Support. People may want to talk with peers about how their definition of crisis has changed over time.

The following role play illustrates this issue:

Mark: Osman, I could use your help on the Crisis Plan. I understand it is a really good thing to have, but I am not sure when I would want my supporters to step in and really take over for me.

Osman: When have they stepped in before and how did that work out?

Mark: Well, lots of times they have stepped in when I really didn't want them to and they insisted, like when they think I am spending too much money or making plans they don't agree with. When I wanted to go back to school they said I was "manic" and had a fit and I didn't appreciate that.

Osman: So it sounds like you want to be really specific with them. I'm kind of curious about what kind of relationship you had with them that they decided when to step in.

Mark: They think they are in charge. I know I need new supporters and that comes along further in the plan. I do want to work with you on that. They certainly don't use Peer Support and that is what I want to get set up. I would like to think with you about the times when I would really need them to step in. Good supporters, I mean. And one thing I thought of was if I was comatose, or if I hadn't moved at all for, say, four hours.

Osman: So if you were comatose or didn't move for four hours, those would be the only times you'd want them to intervene?

Mark: Well, maybe. But I think I need different supporters. The ones I have had before have all been doctors and care providers. In this plan I will be listing peers. I think there are other times when I would want them to get involved. Like if I was spending thousands of dollars that I don't have on things that don't make sense. But I have to be so careful because they are really not in favor of education and I really want to go back to school.

Osman: Do you want to be really specific with them?

Mark: I want to be really specific with them about when they can step in and when they can't. Don't want them to get in the way of me living my life the way I want to live it. I love going to school and studying and I don't want them to get in the way of that. So I would want them to step in if my speech was really slurred, if I couldn't walk, went blind. Or was threatening others or myself. This is hard for me.

Osman: Yes, I can imagine it is! So far you have on this list: if you were comatose, if you hadn't moved for 4 hours, if you were spending thousands of dollars on things that don't make sense (to whom?), if your speech was slurred, if you couldn't walk, went blind or if you were threatening other people or yourself.

Mark: Now that I start thinking about it, if I couldn't walk or couldn't see, I could still make decisions and take action in my own behalf. So this is really tricky. If I can think, I want to be in charge. But describing to someone else when I can think is not easy. What would that be for you?

Osman: I think I'd want to put in something about threatening others and myself as well. Sometimes I say things that I don't really mean literally. I think for me I would want to have a conversation with someone so they really knew what I wanted. We would talk about the kinds of things they're afraid of and what to do if those come up.

Mark: Can you and I have that conversation sometime soon? I think we need to really take our time to figure this piece out. So it may be more time than either of us have now but I definitely want to do it.

Osman: Absolutely!

Discussion Topics

When do you feel you would need and want someone to step in and provide you with intensive care and support? Has that changed over time?

Would it be hard for you to discuss difficult times you have had in the past with peers? Would you feel uncomfortable if you were doing that? How could you deal with that discomfort?

Supporters

The next section of the Crisis Plan is a listing of **supporters** you would want to assist you when you meet the criteria you have stated in the previous section. People have found that including mostly peers and supportive family members and friends on the list is best, limiting the use of care providers who may not be available when needed, and who may be dealing with agency boundary issues, who may have protocols to follow that are not helpful or that would preclude them from following your directives.

Include contact information such as phone numbers and email addresses in your listing, so supporters can be in touch with each other, if that is acceptable to you and to them. Supporters who can meet some of your specific needs can be listed with what they can do, even if they can't fill all of your needs. **In my studies over the years I have found that most people agree that having**

at least five supporters is a good number. It helps assure that someone will be available. Many people have fewer supporters or peers when they start thinking about this. They can work on building the list over time, using resources like *WRAP for Life* (Copeland, M. 2014 Dummerston, VT: Peach Press) and *The Loneliness Workbook* (Copeland, M. 2000 Dummerston, VT: Peach Press) as guides.

Peer Support can help us identify those people we feel most comfortable with. Peers often discuss issues related to finding and keeping supporters, the attributes they appreciate from supporters, supporters who have helped, supporters who have not helped, and supporters who have caused harm or made things worse.

You may want to include a list of people you do not want involved if you are having a difficult time. This could be anybody—a doctor, family member, a care provider. It may be someone who has treated you badly in the past. This is not a time to worry about hurting someone's feelings by not including them. It is about what you have found you need and want and what works for you, what gives you hope and moves you forward.

Discussion Topics:

What attributes do you appreciate in your supporters?

Describe a great supporter and what you liked about them.

Describe situations with supporters that were not helpful or were harmful.

How have you connected with good supporters?

Describe difficulties you have had connecting with possible supporters.

Medications, Supplements and Health Care Preparations

The next section of the Crisis Plan is more straightforward. It is a listing of the medications, supplements and health care preparations you are using, when you use them and why you are using them. Asking yourself, and talking with each other, about why you are using some of these substances, can be sufficient to create change.

Include contact information for your physician and pharmacist, and insurance information. In this section, include a list of medications that are acceptable if medications are needed, and **those that must be avoided**, including your reasons—like side effects or personal preference. You may want to discuss the attributes and liabilities of taking medications or of particular medications with peers, keeping in mind that you are learning together rather than telling each other what you must do.

Discussion Topics

Discuss specific medications and supplements.

Describe good and bad experiences you have had with medications and supplements.

Discuss times when you decided to use medications and why, and times when you have discontinued medications and why.

Discuss efforts to get off of medications after short or long-term use.

Discuss ways to learn about medications.

How can you learn more about medications and supplements?

Why might you want to give your supporters the names of your health care providers, pharmacist and insurance carrier?

Treatments and Complementary Therapies

The next section of the Crisis Plan is Treatments and Complementary Therapies that are acceptable or unacceptable to you, like acupuncture, massage and electroshock, along with any specific instructions about the treatment or therapy. For instance, I have such negative feelings about electroshock that I have instructed my supporters to do whatever they need to do to prevent me from having electroshock, if I am not able to make that decision for myself. I have told my supporters to hire an attorney and go to court to protect me.

Discussion Topics

Discuss the pros and cons of specific treatments and whether or not you would want to use particular treatments.

How has Peer Support affected how you feel about certain medications or treatments?

How do you think you could protect yourself from unwanted or involuntary treatment? How have others protected themselves from unwanted involuntary treatment?

Home Care / Community Care / Respite Center Plan

There are many advantages to having a plan so that you can stay at home or in your community, in even the most difficult times, while continuing to have access to the people, places and things that are important to you—where people know you, understand you and care about you. It may even help you avoid the human rights abuse and violations that occur in impersonal facilities and hospitals.

Many people feel that trauma is at the root of our mental health difficulties and other health issues we are experiencing. To reach out for help or be given what is supposed to be help, and then be further traumatized, is a travesty. Setting up plans so that we can stay safely at home or in the community, and avoid these institutions whenever possible, can keep this kind of thing from happening. Developing these plans takes serious consideration. Working and learning together using Peer Support strategies, each of us can come up with a comprehensive plan that will hopefully carry us through even the worst of times.

Often we feel better more quickly if at home, in our familiar surroundings, with our own things and people who know us close by.

A woman said:

The last time I was in the hospital I was kept in seclusion for the first 48 hours. They brought me food but much of the time I was alone, agitated and scared. Terrible food. Not the kind of food I like to eat. The guy that brought it was rude and scary. It was horrific. I don't know why they did that. It didn't make any sense to me. I didn't do anything wrong. Although maybe they thought it was wrong that I was cutting myself. I thought I was going to get "help." WRONG. I have been working with a couple of peers. We are all developing these plans. I am not going to let this happen to me again.

Crisis Plans can include different options, to help assure that something is possible that will work. It could include: going to a respite center, having family members and friends stay with you in your own home, someplace else you would like to stay and someone else you could stay with. Developing this part of the plan takes careful consideration and extra time. Make it as comprehensive as possible. Avoid assuming others know what you would like and what would be helpful to you without you telling them.

The following role play illustrates using Peer Support when working on this part of the Crisis Plan or Advance Directive.

Jess: I developed the section of my Crisis Plan on staying at home or in the community a long time ago and now I feel like, for me, it is out of date. I wanted to ask you what you have in your plan.

Pat: I have several people that I've gone through this with and we figured out together what we would do if one of us got to the point where we were scaring the others

Jess: What do you mean by scaring people?

Pat: Well, we figured out together what kinds of things were tolerable for each of us and what kinds of things weren't. For example, when I used to cut myself really badly, that was too much for one of my supporters, so we said it would be OK for her to tell the others in my support group.

Jess: I am thinking that when others find out what I might do or have done, it might scare them. I guess probably when I am talking a lot about suicide.

Pat: Yes, I think those discussions are really helpful

Jess: So, if you were doing things that were making your supporters scared, what would you want them to do? That is what I can't figure out, what I would want them to do. Do you have any ideas?

Pat: I think I'd want them to tell me that I was scaring them.

Jess: Then what would you want them to do?

Pat: I think that I'd decide that before it happened, like maybe we'd agree that I would go stay at one of their houses for a few days.

Jess: I think that is what we are doing with this plan. Suppose there is no one who is willing to have you at their house?

Pat: Then I suppose I would be willing to go to a respite center or have a couple of people come and stay with me

Jess: Is there a respite center near you? I don't think there is one near me. I think I would prefer a couple of people who are not "put off" by what I am experiencing to stay with me at my house. I like to be where things are familiar and where I have a lot of my Wellness Tools around.

Pat: Yes, me too, but there is a respite center near me. If no one wanted to stay with me, I guess I would use it.

Jess: What would you want to be able to do when you feel like that?

Pat: I guess I'd want people around me who continued to challenge me but I'd also like some down time, maybe watching movies or going for a bike ride.

Jess: I know I would want to get outside. I feel worse when I don't get outside enough. Can you give me some examples of how you would want people to challenge you? I am not sure I understand that.

Pat: I guess when my friends don't buy into my ideas of "being sick." I hope that people who I trust would be really direct with me (not the "kid glove" thing).

Jess: You mean, you trying to convince them that you're sick and they don't buy that.

Pat: Yes.

Jess: Good for them. Can you give me another example?

Pat: I think when I've been at my worst I get really discouraged and just believe I should be dead. My friends actually say things like, "Do you want my help or do you want me to stop you?" This then puts the responsibility back in my court.

Jess: I get really discouraged too. Could you say a little more about "Do you want my help or do you want me to stop you?" I think it is really important, but I don't quite understand it. If you said, "I don't want you to stop me," would they let you do something to hurt or kill yourself?

Pat: I think everyone is different. Some people might be comfortable with letting me do it but others are not. There is a lot of value in the discussion. And when it's all over, mostly I realize that I don't want to be dead, that I just really want something to change.

Jess: Does being able to talk about it help you feel less discouraged?

Pat: Absolutely. It also makes me clearer about what I need.

Jess: What kinds of things have you needed when this has happened in the past?

Pat: I've needed to run, which I can't do now, so I'll have to think of some new things.

Jess: How about your biking? And I know in the winter you like to ski. Do those things help?

Pat: Yes, sometimes, but I think I may have to find some other things as well.

Jess: What kinds of things are you thinking of?

Pat: Writing, talking to people with my text to speech device, etc.

Jess: This is really good. It's helping me to think in new and different ways.

Discussion Topics

Describe your vision of a Home Care/Community Care/Respite Center Plan that would work for you.

Share experiences you have had using this kind of plan.

If you haven't used plans like these, how do you think they would work?

What are the challenges to developing and using this kind of plan?

What is a respite center? What do you think a good respite center would be like? Are there respite centers in your area?

How do you feel about your supporters abilities to provide the intensive care you might need?

How would plans like this keep you out of coercive and abusive situations?

What would work for you in the worst of times?

Hospital or Treatment Facilities

Part of the object of developing the Crisis Plan, and especially the previous part of the plan, the Home Care/Community Care/Respite Center Plan, **is to avoid the need to go to the hospital**, a treatment facility or an institution. All of the work on WRAP using Peer Support will help make that a reality.

While many people have found that, using WRAP, they have little or no need for these facilities, you may choose to include a list in your Crisis Plan of the hospitals or treatment centers that would be acceptable to you, to help insure that you get what you need and want. **Include a list of hospitals and treatment centers to avoid.** Peers can give you information to include in this list.

Discussion Topics

Describe the hospitals and treatment centers in your area. Are there any that are OK with you? Are there some you would wish to avoid? Why?

Describe a hospital or treatment facility that would work for you.

Describe positive experiences you have had in hospital and treatment facilities. How did they help? What did you learn from them?

Describe negative experiences you had in hospitals and treatment facilities. How did they affect you? How do you think you can protect yourself from having those kinds of things happen to you again?

Help From Others

Most Crisis Plans or Advance Directives that you are asked to fill out when you request services do not ask you what would help, what you would like to learn and what you would like others to do for you. Using Peer Support, you can work together to learn together what works for you and how it can be put into action.

In many cases, our supporters have done for us what they felt was best for us, without asking us for input. This may have included the use of harmful tactics that violate our human rights, like threats, coercion, restraint, isolation and forced medication—tactics that can make us feel much, much worse, at a time when we are most vulnerable. Peer discussions around this issue can help expand our thinking about what is possible at this time.

Consider the following example:

Janet says that when she has been lying on her bed with her head under a pillow for three days, it is an indicator that she needs others to step in. When she described this to her peers, they asked her what she would want them to do in this instance. This was a good question for Janet. No one had ever asked her that before. She thought about it and said that one time she started to feel better, like she could at least get her head out from under the pillow, when Terri, a peer, started playing some of her favorite music. Then Terri asked her if she would like some macaroni and cheese (knowing that was one of Janet's favorite foods). Janet had some macaroni and cheese and began to notice things around her, a beginning, for her. Other people in the group shared similar situations they had experienced, simple safe things that others did for them that began the process of moving forward, like encouraging them to get dressed, going for a short walk with them, watching a favorite television show with them (even having popcorn). One person said that what worked for her was when another person, someone she trusted, just sat quietly and didn't say anything for a time.

As a result of discussion with peers, some of the things others have included in their plans included:

Sit quietly with me.
Ask me what happened.
Ask me what I want and need.
Ask ___________ (name) to come and stay with me.
Arrange opportunities for me to be with peers (name them).
Hold me.
Don't touch me.
Listen to me without giving me any advice.
Listen and listen and listen.
Listen closely to what I say.
Let me express my emotions.
Let me do what I need to do.
Make me macaroni and cheese.
Make me a brownie ice cream sundae.
Get me funny videos to watch.
Play my favorite music.
Cook me a healthy meal.

Include a **list of things people might do for you that would not be helpful and would make you feel worse**, like:

Correcting me
Giving me advice
Nagging
Scolding
Yelling at me
Blaming or shaming me
Teasing me
Trying to divert me with chatter
Inviting lots of people to come over
Playing certain kinds of music (name them)
Describing bad times others have had
Threats or abuse
Restraint

Seclusion

Patti says, "In a crisis, I'd like my supporters to listen without judgment, care without ceasing, comment when I get withdrawn, hug often, and share ideas without telling me what they think is 'best' for me. I hope they would encourage me without being 'Pollyannas,' and take me to a safe place, though not necessarily a hospital setting. I pray they'd be guided by the Crisis Plan section of my WRAP, and not make decisions about me without me."

You can include a list of things you would like to have done for you like:

Buy groceries.
Call my boss and tell him I have a cold.
Pay the rent using my checkbook in the desk.
Feed the pets.
Care for the children. (Anyone who has children needs a carefully designed alternative plan that provides for their care in any emergency—being implemented by people the children know, to assure that the children are comfortable and safe. Other parents who are peers can give input.)

Role Play

Two people discussing the development of a plan to care for their children

Three people discussing things that have helped them move forward when they were experiencing the "signs" they noted at the beginning of their Crisis Plan

Discussion Topics

Describe things that others have done that have helped. How were these things helpful?

Discuss things others have done that did not help. How did you respond? What would have helped you to move forward in this situation?

Talk about things you might be able to do for yourself in times when others think you might not be capable of anything.

Discuss things that you haven't tried at these times, but that you think, if you tried them, they might help.

Talk about how you can let supporters know what would help and what would not help.

Inactivating the Plan

The last section of the Crisis Plan or Advance Directive is **Inactivating the Plan**. This is a list of indicators that let others know that they no longer need to follow the plan—that you are no longer in need of intensive support—the crisis is past. Well-meaning supporters might be reluctant to, or not want to, decrease or stop intensive care. This list might include things like: when I am preparing food for myself, when I am eating at least one meal a day, when I am not afraid to go outside, when I am no longer pacing, or when I return to dressing as I usually do. This is a difficult part of the plan. Discussion with peers or in a WRAP Group will expand the possibilities.

Discussion Topics

What indicators would you include on this list?

Describe situations where people "backed off" when they were no longer needed.

Describe situations where people kept "helping" after it was no longer needed, how that felt to you and how you handled it.

Role Play

Even though you are feeling well, a supporter insists that they need to take you shopping and do your laundry.

A family member insisting that you are not ready to take back care of your child.

Legal Issues

These plans are a guide for people who are willing to provide support at the hardest of times. In some places Advance Directives are legally binding, but in many they are not. However, most supporters are delighted to get this kind of information and do the best they can to do as people wish. Even when the plans are legal, they may not be followed. However, they still give the best chance for people to get the care they need and deserve.

In places where the plans are legal, contact your state Agency of Protection and Advocacy to find out whose signatures you need to have the plan legally recognized. Even where it is not legal, it may be of benefit to get the plan signed by an attorney and several witnesses. This increases the likelihood that others will take it seriously and follow the directions.

When this plan is completed, copies are distributed to supporters. This can be easily accomplished by email. It also helps to hold gatherings of supporters, or to meet with them individually, to talk about the plan and its implementation. Supporters may want to give input on parts of the plan, possible problem areas and suggestions for revisions. The person whose plan it is can decide whether or not they want to include any of these suggestions.

Discussion Topics

What do people know about the legal issues surrounding the use of these plans?

Describe times when the plans have worked or moved people forward and when they have not. What made the difference?

What would increase the likelihood of a plan working?

How could we advocate to insure that these plans are followed?

Chapter 15

Post Crisis Plan

The last section of WRAP is the **Post Crisis Plan.** The Post Crisis Plan was developed several years after the original WRAP. People saw the need for thinking about and planning for that time when we are getting over a hard time and working toward feeling well. This part of the plan differs from other parts of the plan because, while some sections can be addressed or partially addressed in advance, many parts of the Post Crisis Plan may need to be addressed as we are beginning to feel better. The responses will be dependent on our situation at that time.

The Post Crisis Plan form consists of questions we can ask ourselves, either before the hard time (the one we hope will never happen), or when we are beginning to feel better. Even better is if we reach out to a peer supporter to do this with us. Each question or topic can be discussed with either another person or a group. In working with a group on this section of the plan, describe each part of the plan or question as listed below and ask the group for ideas on what might be included in that section. As with the rest of WRAP, people can skip over any questions that aren't meaningful to them or that they don't feel like addressing. The Post Crisis Plan form is in the Appendix.

Serena had just been through a very difficult time, a time she referred to as a crisis. She chose to work her way through the Post Crisis Plan with a peer supporter, Jodie. Their conversations follow each question from the Post Crisis Plan. The questions or statements are bolded. The conversation is in italics.

I will know that I am "out of the crisis" and ready to use this Post Crisis Plan when I am able to:

Jodie asks Serena how she can tell that she is ready to use the Post Crisis Plan. Serena tells Jodie that she has slept at least 7 hours for the last three nights, that she is talking to her supporters (during the crisis she was refusing to speak to anyone), she is taking showers every day and she is eating at least two meals a day. Jodie says that those are similar for her but that another indicator is that she is getting dressed rather than hanging around in her sweats. Serena says that is another indicator for her and adds it to her list.

When I have recovered from this crisis, I would like to feel:

Jodie asks Serena how she would like to feel when she has recovered from this crisis. Serena refers back to the piece she wrote at the beginning of her WRAP that describes what she is like when she is well and says that is how she would like to feel. Jodie asked her if there were any things she would add to that list. Serena said she would like to be more self-confident. She said she felt that her lack of self-confidence got her into the situation that led to the crisis. Jodie said that she has noticed that she has the same issue and that she is looking for ideas on how she could raise her self-confidence as well. She asked Serena about what she thought she would feel like if she were self-confident. Serena said she thought she would feel less anxious and make better decisions for herself. Jodie said those sounded right to her. She also felt that, if she had more self-confidence, she might be able to make some changes in her living situation.

People I want to support me as I work on my recovery:

Serena said that through this hard time she realized that her brother is really not helpful in these situations. He gets too anxious and tries to make her do things that are not helpful. She said that she has found, over the years, that her supporters have changed as she has changed. Jodie agreed with that and said that her list of supporters is the thing that changes most often for her. They talked about being supporters for each other and what they would want from each other.

Will I likely feel safe and be safe at home? ___Y ___N

Jodie said that she used to want people at her house when she got back from the respite center. She has found that has changed for her and she now relishes the solitude at her home when she gets back from being with so many people. She said she used to feel uncomfortable with it, but that now it is actually comforting for her. Serena said she is not quite there yet. Jodie and Serena talked about how they could make that happen.

What will I do to ensure that I will feel and be safe at home?

Serena said that she is concerned that she will not feel safe in her house when she gets home and that is why she wants someone there for her. She talked about a person who lives in her building and goes into people's apartments when they are not there. She says the locks on her apartment don't always work so she feels unsafe, like this person who she is uncomfortable with could come in at any time. Jodie suggested that she contact the landlord to fix the locks and to describe the difficulties she had had to see if she would work with her on this issue. Serena said she wasn't sure she had the confidence she needed to do that but that she would give it a try—that it might be a first step in building her self-confidence.

I would like to stay (where) ______________ for (how long) ___________ before I go home.

Serena said that if the locks weren't fixed, she would rather stay with her sister until that could be taken care of. Jodie asked if there was someone else who could fix the locks if the landlord couldn't do it soon. Serena thought that perhaps she and her sister might be able to do it working together.

I would like _____________ or _______________ to take me home.

Jodie offered to take Serena home or to her sister's. Serena said she really appreciated that and it would work well for her. She also said that, when things were going better, she would be glad to help Jodie out with rides.

I would like _______________ or _______________ to stay with me.

Serena and Jodie had a long conversation about situations in the past where the people who had stayed with her after she got home from respite or the hospital had treated her like she had been "bad." She didn't want that to happen this time as it made her feel ashamed. Jodie asked her if there were people who could stay with her that she didn't think would do that. She was able to name several people from her support group and decided to be in touch with them to see if they could spend an hour or two each day with her for the next few days, giving her time with others and time alone. Jodie said that sounded like a good idea to her and something she might try if she needed to. They had a long conversation about wanting to see a peer each day for a while.

When I get home I would like to _______________ or ______________.

Jodie and Serena had a long talk about the kinds of things they like to do when they have had a rough time and want to move on. They agreed that reviewing their list of Wellness Tools would give them some choices. And that their When Things are Breaking Down Action Plan might be a useful guide for a few days. Through this discussion, they both realized how important this time together was to them and that they would continue to get together at least once a week for as long as they both wanted to—or if that was not convenient they could talk on the phone or online, or get together less often. Jodie suggested that each time they get together, they make a plan for getting together next time so they don't lose the close connection they are both appreciating.

If the following things were in place, it would ease my return:

Jodie said that the last time she was in respite, it helped her a lot that her sister had come in, done her dishes, and tidied up. Serena couldn't think of anyone who could do that for her. Then she thought that perhaps her friend Kim might be willing to work with her on taking care of those things. She said that she would ask her about that when she stopped by later and if she couldn't do it, perhaps they could figure out someone else who could.

Things I must take care of as soon as I get home:

Serena said that she has always been very careful to pay her rent on time and that it was almost due so she would have to pay that as soon as she got home. Jodie described how difficult it was for her when she had things like outstanding bills to pay. They got into a further discussion about how upsetting it is when you can't pay your bills, how that can lead to really bad times and what they might do to keep that from happening.

Things I can ask someone else to do for me:

Jodie asked Serena what she could ask others to do for her. Serena said that this is hard for her, asking others to do things for her. She said she likes to take care of things herself and is often not satisfied when someone else does things for her. Jodie asked her if she felt this was a good thing for her. Serena said there were times when this has really gotten in the way and worsened the situation. Both agreed that this would be difficult for her if she were in a situation where she physically couldn't care for herself. Jodie asked her if there were some small steps she could take to practice allowing someone else to help her when she needed it. Serena thought about that and said she thought she could ask a friend to buy her some groceries, that this might be a start. Jodie said that given this conversation, she was going to be thinking of this as well.

Things that can wait until I feel better or want to take care of them:

Jodie said that for her, the hard part when she was getting better was going back to her exercise class. She said she often waits several weeks before she gets back to that. Serena said it was going to be hard for her to go back to work, that people would ask her where she had been and if she was feeling better. Serena said that she was thinking of making up a "white lie," telling people she had been away rather than telling them she had been at respite. Jodie said that she had done that in the past and that sometimes it works OK. She said the hard part for her was being afraid that people would find out and not understand or ask too many questions.

Things I need to do every day while I am recovering from this crisis:

Jodie said this was a hard piece for her, getting back to doing the things she knew she needed to do to take care of herself. Serena agreed and said that she thought she would try and use her Daily Maintenance Plan every day as a minimal list of things she needed to do and then add in other Wellness Tools as she could. Jodie said that was a great idea and one she might try.

Things and people I need to avoid while I am recovering from this crisis:

Jodie said that the last time she got out of respite, she wanted to avoid everybody. She felt really embarrassed. But her friends kept contacting her and gradually she started having more interactions. Serena felt this might be hard for her as well and thought of one or two peers she could begin to reconnect with, and to continue talking about it and working on it. She thought they should have more conversations about this over time.

Signs that, for me, mean I am be beginning to feel worse—anxiety, excessive worry, overeating, sleep disturbances:

Serena said that, in the past, she has overlooked signs that she was beginning to feel badly again. She said that more than once she has returned to the hospital just a few days after she left. Jodie said that for her, keeping up with all of WRAP made a difference. As soon as she noticed those Early Warning Signs, she took action. Serena thought that was a great idea and shared that she was glad she had WRAP in place before this all happened. She said she wished she had used it more consistently. Jodie talked about having a support group for WRAP users and Serena thought this was a great idea. They agreed to work together to set it up.

Wellness Tools I will use if I am starting to feel worse:

Jodie said that when she notices that she is feeling worse, she refers to the Action Plans for Early Warning Signs and When Things Are Breaking Down. She also said that she goes back to her list of Wellness Tools for more ideas. Serena thought those were good ideas and shared that she was anxious to get back to a good book she is reading, and her exercise routine. She said there was a good concert that she didn't want to miss and asked Jodie if she might attend with her.

What I need to do to prevent further repercussions from this crisis—and when I will do these things:

Serena said she was concerned about her job and didn't want to lose it. She felt that she needed to talk to the Human Resources person at their workplace as soon as possible. Jodie asked her if she would tell the truth about what had happened. Serena said, probably not, that she did not want to jeopardize her job. Jodie concurred. She shared that she had lost a job because she lost too much time to what she used to call "bipolar disorder."

People I need to thank:

Jodie said that after difficult times, she goes out of her way to thank the people who came to her apartment and stayed with her, even when she was very quiet. If she can, she takes them to lunch or makes them lunch. Serena didn't know when she would be up for that. She said she really doesn't like to cook and doesn't have enough money to take people out to lunch. Jodie suggested perhaps having them over to watch a movie and having popcorn might do, or maybe they would just like to hear the "thank you."

People I need to apologize to:

Jodie said that, from time to time, she needs to apologize to someone for calling them repeatedly in the middle of the night and for being rude. She says that since she has used WRAP, she hasn't had to do that. Serena said she couldn't think of anyone she needs to apologize to this time, but she said that, in the past, apologizing might have healed some relationships that she lost.

People with whom I need to make amends:

Jodie said that this question seemed a lot like the previous one. Serena agreed but she did say that she said some things to her mother she wished she hadn't said. She said she would talk to her mother about that and try to heal any breach that had been created. They talked about the intense feelings that came up around this issue.

Medical, legal, or financial issues that need to be resolved:

Jodie said that the last time she was hospitalized, she made a list of things that she must take care of when she got home, or ask someone else to take care of. Serena said that she needed to pay her rent and her credit card bill. She also needed to get a repeat of a thyroid test and a Lyme test. Jodie said it helped her to make a list and Serena thought that might work for her as well. Together they worked on a "to-do" list that included a timeline for when she needed to get things done.

Things I need to do to prevent further loss—like canceling credit cards, getting official leave from work, cutting ties with destructive friends, etc.

Serena told Jodie that when she was feeling really discouraged, she had been rude to one of her closest and best friends, and that now she was feeling really badly about it. She was afraid that she had destroyed the friendship. Jodie said that must feel really awful. She asked Serena if she thought there was anything she could do to resolve that situation. Serena said she wasn't sure but that she wanted to try. She thought she would begin by sending her friend a card, then an email suggesting a phone call if it was all right with her friend. If she didn't hear from her friend she would keep trying with an email or card from time to time. Her goal was for the two of them to get together so they could talk about what happened and the things she was doing to take care of herself so it wouldn't happen again. Jodie thought those things might work and she validated Serena for her efforts.

Signs that this Post Crisis phase is over and I can return to using my Daily Maintenance Plan as my guide to things to do for myself every day:

Jodie said that she always knew she was feeling a lot better when she returned to her exercise class and when she started cooking for herself instead of eating junk food. She said that is when she goes back to using her Daily Maintenance Plan and the other sections of her WRAP. Serena said she thought she would know she was ready to go back to using the other sections of her WRAP when she was sleeping 7 hours each night, getting up at her usual time, and was comfortable talking to her family members on the phone. She said that feeling like she could go back to work part-time was another sign for her.

Changes in the first four sections of my Wellness Recovery Action Plan that might help prevent another crisis:

Jodie said that after each hard time she reviews her WRAP to see if she wants to make any changes. Last time she realized that she needed to be more direct in her When Things Are Breaking Down Plan and include more options that would work for her if she couldn't be physically active. Serena said that she felt that this time she didn't notice a Trigger and didn't respond to it—misinterpreting something a friend said and taking it as a criticism. She felt she would work on that section and perhaps add some new Wellness Tool options there. She also said that she planned to review and revise her whole plan. Jodie said she would be glad to talk about that with her. She also suggested that they might attend a WRAP support group together and that people in the group might have ideas for her WRAP.

Changes in my Crisis Plan that might ease my recovery:

Jodie said that she felt that the Plan for Staying at Home or in the Community was the most important part of the Crisis Plan for her and that she works on it from time to time as her circumstances change. Serena said she hadn't really paid attention to that part of the Crisis Plan and she realizes now how helpful it would have been if she had. She asked Jodie if they could spend some time together on that over the next few weeks.

Changes I want to make in my lifestyle or life goals:

Serena said that this crisis was life-changing for her. She realized how unhappy she was with her job and how much she dreads going to work each day. She said that now she is trying to figure out what to do about it. Jodie said that other members of the support group have worked through issues like this together.

What did I learn from this crisis?

Serena said that she felt she had already addressed this issue. Jodie said there were parts of this Post Crisis section that seemed redundant to her. They agreed to move on.

Are there changes I want or need to make in my life as a result of what I have learned?

Jodie said she liked this question and wondered if Serena had any ideas about this. Serena said that as a result of this crisis she thought there were two things she needed to work on, getting a different job and getting a new living space—away from the man down the hall who keeps bugging her and where there is good maintenance. Jodie said those sounded like great ideas. She told Serena that after one crisis, she started taking some courses at the community college and got training that got her a promotion.

If so, when and how will I make these changes?

Jodie said to Serena, "So when and how are you going to make these things happen?" Serena said she was going to look for a new job right away but she knew that it might take time. She said she was going to set up an appointment with her vocational rehabilitation counselor to get that process started. She also planned to meet with the local housing authority to explore housing options. She thought she could accomplish these things in the next two weeks. Jodie said she thought that was a lot to expect of herself. Serena said she would take that as a challenge.

The Post Crisis Plan can include a **Timetable for Resuming Responsibilities** that others may have had to take over or that did not get done while we were having a hard time. Things like childcare, pet care, your job, cooking and household chores. Like the other parts of the Post Crisis Plan, and of WRAP, this part of the plan will probably benefit from dialogue and Peer Support. Serena felt that she needed a Timetable to resume grocery shopping. She said shopping has always been hard for her and is particularly hard when her self-confidence is low. Following is the sample Plan for Resuming Responsibilities that she and Jodie developed together.

Responsibility: Going grocery shopping

While I am resuming this responsibility, I will ask my sister or Sally to drive me to the grocery store and shop with me.

Plan for Resuming Responsibilities:

Before I go home I will ask my friend Sam to buy me groceries, take them to my house and put them away, so I will have plenty to eat and take care of myself when I get home—enough to last for one week.

First week: I will ask my sister to take me to a small store where I like to get fresh greens.

Second and third week: I will ask my sister to go shopping with me.

Fourth week: I will go and get groceries by myself.

Discussion Topics

Discuss the process of developing a Post Crisis Plan.

People who have developed and used a Post Crisis Plan share their experiences.

The group problem-solves issues people have in using the Post Crisis Plan.

Chapter 16

Living WRAP and Peer Support

This is, perhaps, the most important chapter of this book. WRAP is not just a time period in your life, it is a lifestyle. Now that you have been through a WRAP program, or the process of developing a Wellness Recovery Action Plan using Peer Support, you may have already incorporated some of the things you learned into your life. Your lifestyle may have already changed.

You may want to spend some time every day reviewing your WRAP and taking action when you decide it is needed. Morning, either before or after breakfast, is often a good time to review your WRAP. As you become more familiar with your WRAP, the review process will take less time and you will know how to respond without even referring to your WRAP.

You may have continued to get together with peers on a regular basis to talk about how you are doing. You may be using some of your Wellness Tools from time to time, following your Daily Maintenance Plan and using your action plans. You may find that you are feeling healthier and happier. You may feel that you are relating more positively with your peers, and with other people in your life. And you may be feeling kind of elated like I did when I first began using WRAP.

Some of the things you might notice are that you:

- Feel hopeful instead of fearful about all of your life.
- Know that you have resources you can easily use so that you feel the way you want to feel and do the things you want to do, so that you can move forward in your life.
- Are able to use the things you learned in WRAP in all of your life.
- Are feeling better about your relationships.

- Are feeling connected to others and experiencing mutuality in relationship with others.
- Have more successful interactions and more productive conversations.
- Have choices and options.
- Are open to differing perspectives.
- See the advantage of being supported and giving support.
- Are motivated and moving forward in your life.
- Have people in your life with whom you feel a sense of connection.
- Understand differing perspectives and different life experiences.
- Understand how you see yourself in the world, how that is affecting your life, how that affects the lives of others and what you can do about it.

However, as you keep using WRAP, as much as you want to stick to your plans, and keep up with your relationships with your peer supporters, you may find that it is not always easy, that "life" gets in the way. What can keep you from using your WRAP or from using it as intensively as you know would work for you? Responses to this question from people who are working to live WRAP include:

- Convincing yourself or justifying that you don't have to or need to do the things in your WRAP.
- Getting distracted by other things like email, video games, family issues, and household tasks.
- Have a hard time "getting around to" doing the things that are "good for you."
- Lack of motivation.
- Fatigue.
- Feeling like other things are more important than taking care of yourself.
- Feeling like you are "not worth it."
- Feeling like other people's needs are more important than yours.

You can use any of these responses as a discussion topic with a peer or peers.

Sally feels that the way she sees herself in the world and beliefs about herself get in the way of using her WRAP, things like not valuing herself and telling herself things like "I am not worth it, I don't deserve it, I am not a valuable person, and I don't deserve to be alive." She says that she finds herself thinking that WRAP is not going to work anyway, none of this is going to help, and she's not worth it. This is where Peer Support comes in. Sometimes the negative things we believe about ourselves are hard to change. Sally wishes she felt that she was OK with whoever she is. She believes that this change can happen in a relationship, that a really strong connection with another person, the kinds of connections you have in Peer Support, can do it.

You and your peers will discover many things that keep you from using WRAP and Peer Support. However, there are many strategies that others have used, strategies that work successfully, so that you can learn together and move forward in your lives. Some of the many options of things you can do to support Living WRAP are described in this chapter. There is not significance to the order. Use the strategies that work for you. You and your peer supporters may discover others.

1. Taking Care of Yourself as the Priority

Many people have trouble convincing themselves that they are a priority. This is a big issue for me, probably the biggest issue for me that gets in the way of Living WRAP. How can you convince yourself that taking care of yourself is a priority? Discussing the following comments, and others that you think of, with a peer supporter, may help you to make yourself, and WRAP, a priority in your life.

- The more you are successful and reap the benefits of WRAP and Peer Support, the more incentive it will be to keep doing WRAP and Peer Support.

- Without being judgmental, notice how it feels and works out for you when you don't take care of yourself.

- Do the best you can, and avoid giving yourself a hard time when you don't use WRAP and Peer Support, or when you don't use it as intensively as you wish or feel you need to.

- Being heard and being validated are important to using WRAP. It doesn't help when people tell you that what happened to you is no big deal, that it is not true, to get over it, to forget about it, and to stop talking about it.

Ask them not to say those kinds of negative things to you, and instead to validate what you are feeling and let you know they care about you.

2. Peer Support

People find that continuing to use Peer Support, following the guidelines in this handbook as you are Living WRAP, whether it is with Certified Peer Support Specialists that are connected to an organization or agency, or peers that you have met through your WRAP or other groups, or in the community, is one of the best ways of insuring that you continue to move forward with WRAP. When you have people in your life who support you, working and learning with you as you move forward, where there is mutuality in the relationship, you can learn new ways of doing things, create change, and move forward in your life. This may take time and practice.

Discuss with your peers what each of the following means to you:

- Staying connected
- Exploring how you've come to think about things
- Working with each other to figure out solutions and new ways for each of you to do things that work for you
- Moving together towards figuring out what you want, what you want to do, can do and will do

3. WRAP Thinking

When you first began to learn about WRAP, you may have noticed a different way of thinking, what I call *WRAP Thinking*. Before WRAP, before I knew about the Key Concepts, before I knew about the values of Peer Support, and before I knew there were things I could do for myself and things I could figure out with others, my thinking was limited to "Oh no, this is happening again. Now I won't be able to… and probably… will happen and I will probably have to go to the emergency room and maybe they will give me new meds and probably I will have to stay in the hospital for a while and who knows what might happen there, or I could get in trouble because I lose control over everything."

Now, with WRAP thinking, it's very different. I notice something is different or uncomfortable. I think about what I can do about it, what Wellness Tools I can use, where what I am feeling or experiencing fits in my WRAP, which Action Plan I should follow or what action I need and want to take, and who I can talk to about it. That's WRAP Thinking.

I was meeting with a group of people in Japan who had been experiencing mental health issues for a long time and were entrenched in the mental health system. One man said, "If only, twenty years ago, someone had told me that there are things I can do to help myself." If only he had known about WRAP Thinking.

4. WRAP PALS/Community Links

Some people find that, although they have other people they connect with about WRAP, it helps if two peers that are using WRAP and Peer Support have a more formalized agreement, that they are "WRAP PALS" or "Community Links." Both people would have a WRAP, would agree to getting together regularly to support each other in living WRAP and/or would be available for working together to figure things out when needed. Your WRAP PAL or Community Link could be someone from your WRAP group, the peer supporter you developed your WRAP with or someone else who uses WRAP.

While many people have WRAP PALS informally, WRAP PALS is a program of the Copeland Center for Wellness and Recovery (www.CopelandCenter.com). WRAP PALS stands for **W**ellness **R**ecovery **A**ction **P**lan **P**eers **A**dvocating **L**istening and **S**upporting. It is a model for combining the evidence-based practice of the Wellness Recovery Action Plan curriculum developed by Mary Ellen Copeland (Copeland, M. 2012. Mental Health Recovery and WRAP Dummerston, VT: Peach Press) and Peer Support as described in this handbook and other resources developed by Mary Ellen Copeland (www.WRAPandRecoveryBooks.com) and the Copeland Center for Wellness and Recovery.

Community Links: Pathways to Reconnection and Recovery (Copeland, M., Mead, S. 2016 Dummerston, VT: Peach Press) is a program developed by Mary Ellen Copeland and Shery Mead. It is a voluntary program that matches peers or community members with people who have:

- court orders of non-hospitalization or involuntary commitment
- are dependent on the mental health system for assistance and support; and/or
- feel isolated from their community due to mental health difficulties.

However, anyone who wants to work with a peer on developing and living WRAP can use the Community Links model.

In Community Links programs, peers or community members are trained to assist and support others in developing positive mutual relationships, regaining their independence, integrating themselves into their community, and improving the overall quality of their lives.

This program is based on the findings of the Moving Ahead Research Project (Shery Mead and Mary Ellen Copeland, co-principal investigators, Vermont Real Choices Grant, 2004). In this qualitative research project, the researchers interviewed 28 people who were on orders of non-hospitalization or involuntary commitment. They found that people want to end their dependency on the mental health system, become more fully integrated into the community of their choice, develop the skills and strategies needed for independence, and work toward meeting their own life dreams and goals.

The Community Links Manual is designed for mental health agencies and organizations to use in developing and administering a Community Links Program. It includes the format for a three-day training for people who are in support roles, and downloadable PowerPoint slides and handouts for the training. If you are in an agency or organization working to assist people in their recovery and promote community integration, this manual addresses that need. **However, this manual also contains information that will be useful to anyone who is working with a peer to develop a Wellness Recovery Action Plan using Peer Support and is recommended as a reference. You can get a copy at www.WRAPandRecoveryBooks.com.**

5. WRAP and Peer Support Groups

Participants in WRAP groups and programs often form significant bonds with each other. They may choose to keep meeting, perhaps weekly, every other week, or monthly, or whenever one or several of the members of the group want to set up a meeting to keep their connection strong, to share ideas, successes and challenges, and to provide mutual support.

Groups are often held at peer centers but could be held anywhere that works for the group. WRAP and Peer Support groups can be formal or informal.

- A facilitator is not necessary unless the group decides it wants one. Participants could take turns being facilitators.
- People could decide that each person gets a set period of time to talk—like 10 minutes—to assure that everyone in the group gets time to share, or they may find that the group works well with less structure.

- Support around Living WRAP happens informally as people gather to chat and share their experiences.
- Each meeting can have a specific topic that participants want to focus on at each session. However, most people agree that they want to have time to talk about their specific WRAP-related issues with each other.

6. Key Concepts of Mental Health Recovery and WRAP

Review the Key Concepts of WRAP: Hope, Personal Responsibility, Education, Self Advocacy and Support (Chapter 8) in this book or reach out to a resource like WRAP Plus (Copeland, M. 2011 Dummerston, VT: Peach Press) for in-depth reminders of these concepts, and incorporate them into your life. These concepts were uncovered in peer research in the 1980s, and have continued to be essential for people over time. Work on making them real for you with your peer supporter, your WRAP PAL or Community Link, or in your WRAP Support Group, and practice them every day in all of your life. Each Key Concept is an excellent topic for discussion with a peer or in WRAP and Peer Support Groups.

7. Values and Ethics of WRAP

The ever-powerful Values and Ethics of WRAP were developed through a Peer Support process. Incorporating them into your life will support you in working with your peers, and as you live WRAP. They are discussed in Chapter 6 and there is a Values and Ethics handout in the Appendix that can be copied and used as a guide. Like the Key Concepts, each Value and Ethic is an excellent topic for discussion with a peer or in WRAP and Peer Support Groups.

8. Changing Negative Thoughts to Positive

Most people give themselves negative messages from time to time. Some people do it to themselves a lot. These messages can get in the way of using your WRAP and in moving forward in your life. However, many people have learned, through discussion and practice with their peers, to change negative self-talk to positive. They found that these positive messages supported them in using WRAP, and in moving forward in their lives.

The following exercise can be done with Peers or used in WRAP and Peer Support Groups:

Draw a line down the middle of a sheet of easel pad paper. At the top of the first column write **negative message**. At the top of the other list write **positive**

response. Then people list negative messages they give themselves. Eight or ten is plenty. Then they work together to figure out positive responses that use only affirming words that they can say to themselves instead of the negative messages. Following is an example of such an exercise:

Negative message	Positive response
I can't do WRAP.	I can do WRAP.
I am stuck in my life.	I can move forward in my life.
I will never recover.	I am recovering and moving forward with WRAP.
WRAP won't work for me.	WRAP will work for me.
I am not worth it.	I am worth it.
No one would want to do Peer Support with me.	Many people would like to do Peer Support with me.

People can do this on their own as well, making their personal lists of negative messages with positive responses, using only positive affirming words or images in the responses.

Reinforce the positive messages by discussing them with peers, writing them on sticky notes to stick on prominent places (like a mirror or door) and then reading the positive messages when you see them, repeating them over and over again. You can record them and listen to them from time to time. They could say them out loud or read them to a peer.

9. Affirmations

Repeating powerful statements over and over again may help you incorporate WRAP, and WRAP and Peer Support, into your life. Some of them may be statements you uncovered in the Changing Negative Thoughts to Positive exercise. You can figure out these affirmations with peers or in WRAP and Peer Support groups. Then you can repeat them over and over whenever it works for you, for example, stopped at a traffic light, before going to bed, before getting up, when you can't sleep, when you are meditating, and when you are exercising. I make a list of them on my computer. Then I make copies and keep them in several different places. I write a new list of affirmations whenever I feel it would be best for me.

Affirmations are personal. While you can get ideas on affirmations that might work for you from your peers, only you know which affirmations feel right to you.

Affirmations should always be positive and stated as if they were happening in the present. Examples of affirmations that you might choose to use to support you in Living WRAP are:

I use WRAP to get well and stay well.

I use Peer Support to figure out how to make WRAP work for me.

I do the things on my Daily Maintenance List every day.

I review my WRAP every morning before breakfast.

I have Wellness Tools that I can use to get through difficult times.

I have the resources I need to avoid a crisis.

I revise my WRAP whenever I need to.

I am moving forward in my life with WRAP.

I am learning with my peers.

10. Building Self-Esteem

Some people have trouble using their WRAP because they don't recognize their own value, their own worth and their own strengths. If you think this may be an issue for you, talk about it with your peer supporter or peer supporters. Discussing the following questions with them might help you figure out what you need to do to build your self-esteem and move forward with WRAP:

How can I pay better attention to what I need and want? How can I be sure I pay attention to these needs and these things that I want?

What would it be like to take very good care of myself using WRAP? What would I have to do to take very good care of myself using WRAP?

What gives me the most pleasure in life? How can I have more time in my life to do these things? How can I make sure I do these things? How can WRAP help me to do these things?

How can I accomplish the things I want to accomplish?

What are my strengths? How can I use them to keep me going forward with WRAP?

How can I use my talents and abilities as I work on my WRAP? How do I feel about myself and moving forward with WRAP when I spend time with people who treat me well? How do I feel about myself and moving forward in my life when I do good things for other people?

How does my living space affect how I feel about myself and influence moving forward with WRAP? Are there changes I want to make in my living space that would support moving forward? How could I make these changes happen? Does my living space honor me as a person? If not, what could I do to my living space so that it honors me as a person?

Is there some skill I could improve or some new skill I could learn that would help me feel better about myself and support me in living WRAP moving forward in my life?

Are there things I could do for others that would improve my self-esteem? If so, what would they be? How could I make them happen? How would this support living my WRAP?

What do I need to do to treat myself well?

With your peers you could each share:

- Five or more of your strengths and how they support living WRAP
- Five or more things you admire about yourself and how they support living WRAP
- The five greatest achievements in your life so far and how they support living WRAP
- Ten things you have accomplished and how they support living WRAP
- Ten ways you can treat or reward yourself and how that would support living WRAP
- Ten things you can do to make yourself laugh and how that would support living WRAP
- Ten things you could do to help someone else and how that would support living WRAP
- Ten things you can do that help you feel good about yourself and how that would support living WRAP

11. Meditation or Relaxation Exercises

Peers often like to do relaxation or meditation exercises together and then discuss their experience. They find it supports them in Living WRAP. You can find these exercises in the WRAP resources (www.WRAPandRecoveryBooks.com), in other self help books, on DVDs and online. You could use the following meditation that deals with building self-esteem. You could have someone read this exercise to you while you relax, or you could record it slowly on a recorder or on your phone and then play it back to yourself.

> Make yourself comfortable. Close your eyes if you are comfortable doing so. Take several deep breaths (pause for about a minute). Now focus all your attention on your right leg. Let your right leg relax completely. Feel the relaxation. (pause) Now focus all your attention on your left leg. Let your left leg relax completely. Feel the relaxation. (pause) Now focus all your attention on your lower back. Let your lower back relax completely. Feel the relaxation. (pause) Now focus all your attention on your upper back and shoulders. Let your upper back and shoulders relax completely. Feel the relaxation. (pause). Now focus all your attention on your left arm. Let your left arm relax completely. Feel the relaxation. (pause) Now focus all your attention on your right arm. Let your right arm relax completely. Feel the relaxation. (pause) Now focus all your attention on your head. Let the muscles in your head, your scalp, your forehead, your cheeks, your jaws and even your neck relax completely. Feel the relaxation. (pause) Notice the feelings of relaxation all over your body. You feel comfortable and peaceful. Now listen to the following statements about yourself: You are a wonderful person. You have many strengths, talents and abilities. You have accomplished many good things in your life including developing and using WRAP and you will accomplish many more. You are proud of yourself for having the courage to keep going and keep using your WRAP in even the most difficult times. You are a winner. Notice how this feels in your body. Stay with these good feelings for several moments. Tell yourself: I have a right to feel this way about myself all the time. WRAP will support me in doing that. (long pause) Bring your attention back to the room.

Talk with your peers about whether doing meditations like this one would be good Wellness Tools for you and if such a practice would support Living WRAP and moving forward in your life.

12. Assessing Your Daily Life

Making some lifestyle changes may make it easier for you to implement WRAP and move forward in your life. Consider the following questions and review them with your peer supporters to see if there are changes you need and want to make. Figure out, with your peers, how to make these changes. You and your peers will probably uncover other issues you want to address as you assess your life.

Is your lifestyle too hectic and chaotic?

Are you always taking care of others and not taking care of yourself?

Do you try to do too much every day?

Do you take on more than you should?

Do you have more things than you need?

Do all these things make your life difficult to manage?

Are there people in your life that make your life chaotic?

Do you wish you had more fun?

Do you need to make some lifestyle changes? Is so, how and when are you going to make these changes?

13. Barriers and Challenges

You may have barriers and challenges in your life that make it very difficult for you to use your WRAP and move forward in your life, even after you have completed your WRAP. For instance, you may be institutionalized, homeless, living in an area or region that is not safe, in prison or jail, have poor housing, or living with people who treat you badly or who need a lot of care. You may not have access to health care or health insurance, you may have had great loss in your life, or you may have been traumatized by severe fire, bad weather or geologic events that make it difficult for you to move forward. You may be disabled or have a serious and painful illness. You may be addicted to drugs or alcohol. You may not have any money or not enough money to provide you and your family with the necessities of life. You may hear voices, have psychosis, be paranoid, or have thoughts of hurting yourself. This list could go on and on. Any of these could be excellent excuses for not using WRAP and for not moving forward in your life.

And yet many, many people in dire circumstances have used WRAP, Peer Support or WRAP and Peer Support together to move forward in their lives. The first person I knew to use Peer Support to move forward in her life was my mother. This was back in the early 1950s, before WRAP, before anyone recognized the value of Peer Support, and before people understood that recovery from serious mental health issues was possible. My mother had been in an institution for eight long years before a volunteer, a peer, starting listening to her and she started sharing. As she tells it, she talked and talked and talked. And then she noticed she was feeling better. The sadness that she had lived with for so many years was going away. So she started gathering other "patients" in the institution together and encouraging them to talk to each other and listen and listen and listen, to work together and learn together so they could get their lives back. And before long, my mother was discharged and went on to lead a rich and successful life.

My mother is the first person I heard about. Now I have been doing this work for almost 30 years, and I have met lots and lots of people in all kinds of situations, situations like those I listed above. And many, many of them have used Peer Support and WRAP to make it possible for them to learn together and move forward in their lives. I believe that moving forward in one's life is possible for everyone, no matter how dire their circumstances.

Working with a peer supporter, you can learn together, develop and live a WRAP that works for both of you and, like my mother, move forward in your life.

With your peer supporters, you can address the following topics, learn together and figure out how to move forward in your lives.

What issues get in the way when I try to live WRAP and move forward in my life?

What Wellness Tools could I use to overcome this barrier or to meet this challenge?

What goals would I like to set for myself around living WRAP and meeting this challenge?

What first steps could I take to overcome this barrier or meet this challenge?

When could I begin taking those steps?

Discuss with your peers other issues you might need to address to overcome these barriers and challenges, use your WRAP and move forward in your life. Then, work with them over time to figure out the answers and take action in your own life to meet your goals and be able to be the way you want to be and do the things you want to do.

At WRAP Facilitator Training we do an exercise called "Problem Solving" that you may want to do with your peers. It helps to have an easel pad and markers so the responses can be recorded and given to the person with the issue. One person shares their problem or issue. Then peers share possible solutions. One person records the responses. The person with the problem does not interrupt with reasons why the suggestion might not work. All of the ideas are written down. Then the sheet is given to the person and they can consider them, talk to peers about them and decide which actions they will take so they can Live WRAP and move forward in their lives. For instance, a person might share the following problem: It is hard for me to live WRAP because I have been in jail for three months. Then other people in the group share ideas they have about how this person could Live WRAP.

Shery Mead shares the following example of how Peer Support can get you past times when it is hard to use your WRAP, when you can think up many excuses for not living your WRAP:

> I am having trouble leaving the house. I know I should get out and go to the gym, maybe do some shopping, but all those issues about safety come up for me. I might tell myself that I might fall, or maybe it's just too cold out, or my kitchen is so nice and cozy. I could do this another day. Pretty soon, I've convinced myself that staying home just one more day won't hurt anyone. Then my friend calls and says, "Let's go to the gym. I'll pick you up and we can go together."
>
> So this time I go. She has gotten me out the door, which is always step one. And I go and feel pretty good. What happens next time?
>
> The next time comes along and I think it will be easier. After all, I felt better the last time I went but then the time comes and I figure I went with my friend a week ago anyway, so why do I need to go again?
>
> This time the friend can't go but she calls me on the phone. Supposing she asks me whether I'm going to the gym and I say, "Well, no." If she says, "Well, what about your WRAP?" Chances are I'll shut down and either lie or I'll go along with her for a while, very clear that when she hangs up, I'll continue to do what I've always done. Or I'll go just to please her, and secretly feel resentful.
>
> But what if she says instead, "I remember you told me that sometimes you have a hard time getting out of the house, and I'm wondering if now is one of those times?"

Depending on how sincere she sounds, I may open up and say, "Yes."

Now comes the tricky part for my friend. Supposing she says, "Well, what do you need to do in order to leave the house?" I may very well go back to disconnecting. This is because she started with moving towards before we had really talked about the situation, before we got the bigger picture. When we start a conversation with problem solving we often don't get the bigger picture and chances are we can only come up with the ideas that we already have.

So we can try something different. What if she shares her own story of not being able to do something she knew she should do, and then asks me if it is anything like that for me. Now I have something to compare it to and it may give me some new ideas. Just this small connection may start a new conversation and together we figure out the kinds of things that may work for both of us. We think of options instead of excuses.

14. Anchoring

Anchoring refers to locking into the good feelings that you noticed when you were intensively using your WRAP, remembering times when you felt really well, and *anchoring* it—holding on to that place so you can go back to it when you need to, to remember it, visualize it, and feel it. I often go back to a time when I was on a beautiful, warm beach. And a time when I supported a friend and it felt really good. You can find places on your body to anchor feelings and events, kind of like a touchstone—tying things to something. Your touchstone could be a place or a thing, or your hair, or the center of the chest, or your right knee. Anchoring is a Wellness Tool.

15. Doing the Things You Love to Do

Hopefully your Wellness Toolbox and your WRAP Action Plans are filled with the things you love to do, things that are fun for you, things that make you feel good when you do them, things that lift your spirits, things that help you feel better and keep you well. Years ago, when I was experiencing a lot of mental health distress, I realized that I wasn't using my extra time or free time, time when I didn't have other responsibilities, to do things that I love to do. It had been so long since I had done the things that I love to do that I couldn't even remember what they were. If this is true for you, a good way to figure out what they are is to discuss it with your peers. As you have these conversations, you will get more and more ideas of things you love to do. (Some people may even share things you know you wouldn't want to do.) Then make doing these things you love to do a part of your WRAP. Talk to your peer supporters about how it is going.

When I first became aware for myself of how long it had been since I had done things that I love to do, I did lots of reminiscing, talking about good times I had in the past, some of them very, very long ago. I tried a lot of things. Some of them felt great. Some I decided I would rather leave behind. With ideas and encouragement from peers, I tried things I had never tried before. Some I enjoyed and some I didn't. For some, once was enough. Others I did several times or many times before I was really clear on how they worked for me. And I found that some things worked for a time and then I was ready to move on to something else. These are the things that make up the rich fabric of your life.

My own list of things I do for fun includes things that I do with others and things that I do alone. The things I do with others include my exercise class, hiking, going out for lunch, and inviting a friend to my house to catch up. My alone things include gardening, cooking, playing the piano, quilting, drawing and reading a good book. I also enjoy taking an educational course either on line or, if I can find one, in my community. Special activities, like going to the movies and concerts and going out to dinner, are fun activities that I often share with peers.

Examples of Living WRAP

Mary Ellen's Story

> *Today I notice that I am feeling somewhat anxious, not how I describe myself in the "What I am Like When I am Well" section of my WRAP. And I recall that I didn't sleep too well last night. And that I am upset about my granddaughter's recent hospital stay. Instead of letting it go, not thinking about it or not focusing on it, I refer to my Triggers and Early Warning Signs Action Plans. And I do the things or some of the things listed there, like spending an hour working on an art project, taking the dog for a walk in the park, and calling a peer supporter who gives me plenty of time to look at things from different angles. And if none of them feels just right, or I need something more, I go to my Wellness Toolbox and choose to do a few more things. Things like working on a quilting project, watching a favorite show on TV and making myself some popcorn (a comfort food for me). I use my Wellness Tools until I feel a whole lot better and can get on with what I need or want to do.*

Jack's Story

Jack, a man who had been a service user in the mental health system for a long time, noticed he was having a hard time getting up in the morning and going to work. Instead of going to the doctor and asking for a medication change, he calls Bill, who is a peer, and asks if they can spend the evening together watching a video, talking and going for a walk. During the day he uses his Action Plan, doing his relaxation exercises at least three times and avoiding eating the sugary foods that always make him feel worse. The next day he plans a get together after work with a peer supporter and with his sister who always makes him laugh, goes for a run, and eats a healthy dinner before listening to some of his favorite music and heading off to bed. Things are starting to look up for Jack.

Sophie's Story

Sophie goes for her annual physical and finds out that her blood test reveals that she is in the pre-diabetic range. She knows that there is a history of diabetes in her family, and her father died of complications from diabetes when he was younger than she is now. She educates herself enough to know that early detection and a healthy lifestyle can keep her from going any further down the road of having a chronic disease. She makes an appointment with a naturopath and together they create a nutritional diet plan. Her Wellness Toolbox now includes a specific exercise plan and a low carbohydrate/low sugar/high protein diet. She signs up for a yoga class to keep her stress level down. She feels confident that by using these Wellness Tools, she will not only be able to avoid becoming diabetic, but even be able to get her blood sugar back into a normal range.

Peter's Story

Peter had been having a difficult time adapting to life now that he is older and can no longer work. At first he felt sad, bored and even fearful about his future much of the time. Then he spent some time with a peer supporter. They talked about Peter's work, which had been all encompassing. When the peer supporter shared with Peter that retirement had actually been hard for him too, Peter got curious. He started thinking about things he had enjoyed earlier in his life. In their conversations, Peter remembered that when he was in college he enjoyed playing the guitar. He arranged for his daughter to come by with her guitar. He played his daughter's guitar and had so much fun he decided to get himself a guitar and take some lessons, perhaps from his daughter. That got him thinking about other things he used to do, before life got so busy. He began restoring an old vehicle in his garage, reading mysteries and doing some gardening. His peer supporter told him about WRAP and together they began to work on a Wellness Toolbox that would include the things that he found helpful.

Joe's Story

For several months, Joe had been working with his newly developed WRAP as his guide to daily living, using his Action Plans as he made his way through harder times and using Wellness Tools to make his life interesting and enjoyable. He now feels ready to make some changes in his work situation. He is feeling hopeful and likes "moving forward." He is considering taking some evening courses to update his skills before applying for a different job. As he considers this, he arranges a time to get together with several of his peers. He tells them what he is thinking of doing. Several of his peers give suggestions of possible places he might take these courses and some of the benefits of each. They ask him questions that help him decide if this is really a step he wants to take. They talk together about how this might affect his lifestyle and his relationship with his partner. They also talk about his current job, what works for him and what doesn't. They talk about the value of his current flexible hours and how he would feel about a job where there were set times. During this conversation, Sharon interjected that this was helping her see her own situation in new ways. She asked Joe if seeing himself as a person without resources was getting in the way for him. Joe left the conversation with a lot of positive things to think about, knowing that, as he made his decisions and took action, he could rely on WRAP and Peer Support to be with him along the way.

Stella's Story

Stella had been in a state institution for many years. She felt like her life was on hold and she lived with feelings of constant deep despair. She didn't know what to do to get herself out of this horrific situation, which started with deep sadness after the loss of her spouse. Repeated trials on various psychiatric medications left her feeling worse and worse. She felt like her mind didn't work any more and that her behavior was out of her control. She had no friends and felt abandoned by her family. She was surprised when Peggy came to visit her and together, using Peer Support, they developed a Wellness Recovery Action Plan. Sometimes they didn't get much work done on the WRAP because they had so much to talk about. This was the first person she felt that she had connected with in a very long time. She began doing small things for herself, like making her bed, going to activities, smiling at people and even asking others how they were doing. She even began having conversations with people, something she hadn't done for a long time. They were short at first but gradually, and with ongoing practice with Peggy, she found she could be engaged with others more and more. Working together with Peggy and other peers, and with WRAP as her guide, she came up with a plan that would move her forward. She discussed it with her social worker who was supportive. Finally she could see a way out of the institution and back to life.

Sam's Story

Sam was in his early 20s. He felt like he was having a hard time getting on with his life. He had been in treatment for addiction issues and was just beginning to feel like he had some control over his life when he began to work with one of his peers, Fred, on developing WRAP plans. Throughout the WRAP process they had lively discussions about each section, benefitting from their mutual experiences and their enjoyment of time together. They learned together as they proceeded with what at first had seemed like it would be an arduous task, but that became rewarding and enjoyable over time. After they completed their Plans, they continued to spend time together sharing their dreams and their accomplishments and doing something fun, like going to a ball game, from time to time.

Finally

Over time, working with WRAP and Peer Support, whatever your role, you will have your own story to share. Everything in this book has been learned from years and years of learning from people like you, people with lived experience. I urge you to share that story, to send it to info@WRAPandRecoveryBooks.com so we continue this process of learning from each other, a process that has been tremendously powerful and effective.

Appendices

Fundamentals of WRAP and Peer Support

Appendix 1

Values and Ethics of WRAP and Peer Support

1. WRAP groups and WRAP and Peer Support focus on hope.
2. Self-determination, personal responsibility, empowerment, and self-advocacy are key components of WRAP, Peer Support, and WRAP and Peer Support together.
3. In all WRAP groups, Peer Support groups and related programs, everyone is equal and the relationships we have with each other are mutual. Every person is treated with dignity, compassion, mutual respect, and unconditional high regard; as unique, special individuals, including complete acceptance of diversity with relation to culture, ethnicity, language, religion, race, gender, age, disability, sexual identity, and "readiness" issues.
4. There are "no limits" to recovery.
5. Every aspect of WRAP and Peer Support is voluntary.
6. The person who is developing their WRAP and using Peer Support is the expert on him or her self.
7. The focus is on personal strengths and away from perceived deficits.
8. The use of diagnostic and medical language is limited or avoided.
9. The emphasis is on the many different strategies (Wellness Tools) that are simple and safe, and away from strategies that are invasive or that may have serious, devastating or long-lasting side effects.

10 It is recognized that every person has had traumatic things happen to them in their lives, the kinds of things that cause mental health issues.

Responses to traumatic events, even though they may have happened in the distant past, are normal, and are not signs of "mental illness" and are not "mental health issues."

Appendix 2

WRAP Forms

My Wellness Tools

What I'm Like When I'm Well

What I Need to Do Every Day

Things I Might Need to Do

My List of Triggers

My Triggers Action Plan

My Early Warning Signs

My Early Warning Signs Action Plan

My Signs That Things Are Breaking Down

My Action Plan for When Things Are Breaking Down

Crisis Plan

Part 1— What I'm like when I'm feeling well

Describe yourself when you are feeling well.

____

____

____

____

____

Part 2— Signs That Others Need to Take Over

Describe those signs that would indicate to others that they need to take over responsibility for your care and make decisions in your behalf.

____

____

____

____

____

Part 3— Supporters

List those people you want to take over for you when the signs you listed above are obvious. They can be family members, friends or health care providers. Have at least five people on your list of supporters. You may want to name some people for certain tasks like taking care of the children or paying the bills and others for tasks like staying with you and taking you to health care appointments.

Name _______________________________________
Connection/role____________________Phone number ______________
Name _______________________________________
Connection/role____________________Phone number ______________
Name _______________________________________
Connection/role____________________Phone number ______________

Name ____________________
Connection/role ____________________ Phone number ____________________
Name ____________________
Connection/role ____________________ Phone number ____________________
Name ____________________
Connection/role ____________________ Phone number ____________________

There may be health care providers, family members, or friends who have made decisions that were not according to your wishes in the past. They could inadvertently get involved if you don't include the following:

I **DO NOT** want the following people involved in any way in my care or treatment:

Name ____________________
Why you do not want them involved (optional)

____

____

Name ____________________
Why you do not want them involved (optional)

____

____

Name ____________________
Why you do not want them involved (optional)

____

____

Settling Disputes Between Supporters

You might like to include a section that describes how you want possible disputes between supporters settled. For instance, you may want to say that a majority need to agree, or that a particular person or two people make the determination.

____

____

Part 4— Medication and Health Care

Physician ____
Phone Number ____

Physician ____
Phone Number ____

Physician ____
Phone Number ____

List the medications you are currently taking and why you are taking them. Include the name of the doctor and the pharmacy.

____

____

____

____

____

List those medications you would prefer to take if medications or additional medications became necessary, and why you would choose those.

____

____

____

____

____

List those medications that would be acceptable to you if medications became necessary and why you would choose those.

____

____

List those medications that must be avoided and give the reasons.

____

____

Part 5— Treatments

List treatments that help you feel better and when they should be used.

____

____

____

____

____

List treatments you would want to avoid

____

____

____

____

____

Part 6— Home/Community Care/Respite Center

Set up a plan so that you can stay at home or in the community and still get the care and support you need.

____

____

____

____

____

____

Part 7— Treatment Facilities

List treatment facilities where you prefer to be treated or hospitalized if that becomes necessary.

____

____

List treatment facilities you want to avoid

Part 8— Help From Others

List those things that others can do for you that would help you feel better or make you more comfortable.

List those things you need others to do for you and who you want to do what.

List those things that others might do, or have done in the past, that would not help or might make you feel worse.

___

___

___

Part 9— Inactivating the Crisis Plan

Describe signs, lack of signs or actions that indicate supporters no longer need to use this plan.

___

___

___

___

___

You can help assure that your Crisis Plan will be followed by signing it in the presence of two witnesses. It will further increase its potential for use if you appoint a durable power of attorney.

I developed this plan on (date) __________ with the help of ________________ ________________________.

Any plan with a more recent date supersedes this one.

Signed ________________________________
Date ______________

Witness ________________________________
Date ______________

Witness ________________________________
Date ______________

Attorney ________________________________
Date ______________

Durable Power of Attorney (If you have one)

____

Phone number ________________

My Post Crisis Plan

If you've been in a Crisis, the Post Crisis Plan is a list of questions that will help you figure out what you need to do to get past the Crisis. Familiarize yourself with this section when you develop the rest of your WRAP, and complete it when you are recovering from a Crisis. That is when you will know what you really need and want. Using and living WRAP will make this process easier for, easing your recovery and assuring you that you will soon be using your Daily Maintenance Plan again. I will know that I am "out of the crisis" and ready to use this Post Crisis Plan when I:

____

____

How I would like to feel when I have recovered from this Crisis:

(You may want to refer to the first section of your Wellness Recovery Action Plan—What I am Like When I am Well. This section may be different from what you felt like before—your perspective may have changed in this Crisis.)

____

____

Post Recovery Supporters List

I would like the following people to support me if possible during this Post Crisis time:

Who:	Phone number:	What I need them to do:
________________	______________	______________________
________________	______________	______________________

If you are being discharged from a treatment facility, do you have a place to go that is safe and comfortable? ___ yes ___ no

If not, what do you need to do to insure that you have a safe, comfortable place to go?

____

____

If you have been hospitalized, your first few hours at home are very important. Will you feel safe and be safe at home? ___ yes ___ no

If your answer is no, what will you do to insure that you will feel and be safe at home?

____

____

I would like ____________________ or ____________________ to take me home.

I would like ____________________ or ____________________ to stay with me.

When I get home I would like to ______________________________ or ______________________________.

If the following things were in place, it would ease my return:

____

____

Things I must take care of as soon as I can:

____

____

Things I can ask someone else to do for me:

____

____

Things that can wait until I feel better:

____

____

Things I need to do for myself every day while I am recovering from this Crisis:

____

____

Things I might need to do every day while I am recovering from this Crisis:

____

____

Things and people I need to avoid while I am recovering from this Crisis:

____

____

Signs that I may be beginning to feel worse:

(examples: anxiety, excessive worry, overeating, sleep disturbances)

____

____

Wellness Tools I will use if I am starting to feel worse:

(star those that you must do, the others are choices)

____

____

Things I need to do to prevent further repercussions from this Crisis—and when I will do these things:

____

____

People I need to thank:

Person:	When I will thank them:	How I will thank them:

People I need to apologize to:

Person:	When I will apologize:	How I will apologize:

People with whom I need to make amends:

Person: When I will make amends: How I will make amends:

____

____

Medical, legal, or financial issues that need to be resolved:

Issue: How I plan to resolve this issue:

____

____

Things I need to do to prevent further loss: (canceling credit cards, getting official leave from work if I left without notice, cutting ties with destructive people, etc.)

____

____

Signs that this Post Crisis phase is over and I can return to using my Daily Maintenance Plan as my guide to things to do for myself every day:

____

____

Changes in the first 4 sections of my Wellness Recovery Action Plan that might help prevent a Crisis in the future:

____

____

Changes in my Crisis Plan that might ease my recovery:

____

____

Changes I want to make in my lifestyle or life goals:

____

____

What did I learn from this Crisis?

____

____

Changes I want or need to make in my life as a result of what I have learned:

____

____

When and how will I make these changes:

____

____

Timetable for Resuming Responsibilities

Develop plans for resuming responsibilities that others may have taken over or that did not get done while I was having a hard time (things like child care, pet care, my job, cooking and household chores).

SAMPLE

Responsibility: <u>going back to work</u>

Who has been doing this while I was in Crisis: <u>co-workers</u>

While I am resuming this responsibility, I need (who):

<u>Jane and Eric</u> to <u>help with record keeping</u>

Plan for resuming:

Steps:

- in three days go back to work for 2 hours a day for five days
- for one week go back to work half time
- for one week work ¾ time
- resume full work schedule

Responsibility:

Who has been doing this while I was in Crisis: ____________________________
While I am resuming this responsibility, I need (who):
______________________________ to ______________________________________

Plan for resuming:

____

____

Responsibility: ____

Who has been doing this while I was in Crisis: ____________________________

While I am resuming this responsibility, I need (who):
______________________________ to ______________________________________

Plan for resuming:

____

____

____

Appendix 3

Using Technology for Peer Support

When I first began doing this work, I had a primitive computer that I used to compile data from handwritten surveys that I sent out by snail mail to people all over the country, and eventually all over the world. Now we have technology that allows us to connect to people everywhere almost instantly. Some people have found this to be an effective form of Peer Support.

To find out more about this, I asked people on Facebook and through my email list if they use electronics for Peer Support, if so, how they do it, and how it works for them. Following is a listing of what I heard from some of them. I edited their responses for clarity, but not knowing your needs or circumstances and what might "speak to you," I chose to leave most of it, just as it was written to me. There are some opinions that are expressed that I don't necessarily agree with.

Sinead says she had severe Post Natal Depression. She says she used Facebook and Twitter to help other mothers recover by offering support/advice. She says there are lots of online support groups and she has seen people who are really struggling being helped by these groups. She says that some people don't have anyone else to talk to. On Twitter many groups link up and share ideas.

Once they get into it, they often have a real desire to help others. It works really well.

Debbie says: "I am agoraphobic so technology is vital to me." She says she is able to keep in contact with family and friends, and touch base with counselors. She finds it much easier to send an email than to make a phone call. She gets a lot of support and information online. She also enjoys face-to-face contact because she is challenging herself to "even go there." But without the online contact, she feels like it would be so easy for her to become even more secluded and drop out of life.

Michel is a WRAP Facilitator from The Netherlands. He finds that it is often easier to talk with someone on social media. For him, it takes some shame away and if you don't want to go outside, you can still be in touch with people. It keeps you in control! He says you can connect or disconnect with people whenever and wherever YOU want. It doesn't feel to him like total isolation anymore. He says you keep in touch with the world around you and you can get connected very easily with others around the world to share possibilities!

Amber says she uses Facebook, Skype, FaceTime, Snap Chat, and Glide to stay in contact with family and friends both near and far.

Tabitha works in the mental health field and serves in a recovery ministry. She says that although she sees her "recovery family" often, they communicate through Facebook throughout the week. She uses her personal page to share Wellness Tools, offer encouragement, and provide support, and will often start a conversation that progresses into a phone call or a visit. They use a Facebook "secret" group that provides a safe environment where people can share without having their comments seen by the public.

Kathleen feels that any way you can relate to others, share what works and eliminate the lonely feeling that isolates, is great support. She finds that a face-to-face interaction increases the chance of interruption and gives you less time to think of what you really want to say. She can communicate with less stress and more accuracy by text. A phone call with someone you trust also works for her. She says that trust is key.

Joy says that she prefers face-to-face contact because she likes to be touched and likes to see expression. She says technology is great but it is definitely more difficult and less personal.

Patty also likes "face-to-face" contact. She says it makes it easier for her because she likes the personal closeness. She feels that she can't get that from technology.

Lindy likes face-to-face contact with people but does feel that she can access it through Face Time and other social media. She has grown to appreciate the social media more as it seemed to allow her to build confidence and process information as she was comfortable. She feels it's important to provide options for people. That way more people have the ability to connect at their own pace.

Carla likes technology. However, she also feels there is nothing better than face-to-face contact. She says that reading body language and making direct eye contact is so valuable when connecting with people.

Diana says she uses everything: Texting for quick questions or support ("I'm craving a cigarette. I text someone to get the thought out of my head. The action of using my fingers and thumbs is distracting."); Hangout and Skype for loved ones who live too far away to visit a lot, and to talk to her grandchildren; Facebook and Facebook support groups for meeting people from all over the world and sharing ideas for fun and difficulties; and Email for support in personal things ("with peers who I've met through trauma and hearing voices work"). Diana make sure she balances her time with technology with face-to-face time. She says she tends to like being alone a "wee bit" too much sometimes, so she makes sure she's out and about, even if she is simply visiting her neighbor or family and friends who live closer.

Amey says, "I use Facebook support groups for problem solving and to gain different perspectives and clarity for any thoughts or feelings I may be having. Since my face-to-face supporters don't always understand what I go through, it's nice to have another outlet for my thoughts. It's always nice to know that people from all over the world can relate and are able to provide encouragement and ideas when I am not feeling well."

Jaimi says that there are some great apps. She likes Optomism, which is for tracking mood and reminds her to use her coping skills.

Jessie says that technology does not satisfy the "people contact value." It just helps pass the time and at times helps, especially when people are separated by miles. It does not compare to having face-to-face contact. Just having someone sit with you and listen is most important.

Tracey says, "Sometimes you want to keep in touch but not face-to-face. Face-to-face can feel too invasive and exhausting when you are going through a bad time. But knowing there is some communication is better than none. Typing a response and getting one back can be very therapeutic for me. I can actually see written words and these responses from friends are like affirmations that someone is glad that I exist. 'Emoticons' can be useful when you don't know what to say. Sometimes it is better than face-to-face."

Rebecca shares a worst-case scenario. She started using Facebook to catch up with friends. While waiting, she'd play games. She caught herself ignoring instant messages because she was so into the game. Hours turn to days, resulting in game addiction and anti-social behavior. She has decided that a phone call or face-to-face contact is a better way to interact. She feels that a lot gets lost in translation with typing due to guessing expression and intent, not to mention the speed of typing, electronic glitches and spell check "mess-ups."

Linda uses social media a lot and likes it, but not as much as face-to-face contact. However, when face-to-face contact is not possible, social media is good for her. It helps her to feel less isolated.

Robert uses social media a lot, and also finds face-to-face support very helpful. He uses closed Facebook groups for specific issues, and has made individual connections within those groups with people with whom he feels he can share in more detail. He has a "local-ish" support group that he can go to weekly that is about specific aspects of his recovery, and he has built various friendships over time that are also helpful. For him it is a combination of technology and face-to-face support.

Angela says she doesn't know if texting counts as social media, but it has become her personal favorite for reaching out to her support network.

Aine says that quality face-to-face interaction is good but not always possible. Social media (Facebook and Twitter) allow her to connect to other survivors of psychiatric abuse, to gain knowledge, to network, to educate herself, to learn about WRAP, to build back confidence and to try to help others have informed consent (something she never had). "It was a life-saver on some level in the loneliness of the 'real world' after what happened to me 7 years ago."

On the downside, she feels that social media can be used by mental health charities and those who benefit from the "illness model" to encourage people to claim they are "mentally ill" when they may just be going through things like emotional distress, and the effects of the drugs. She feels that people should not take on the "mental illness" label lightly as it has many implications for a person's life. She says, "Giving someone a psychiatric diagnosis is an immensely powerful act which has profound implications for their identity, relationships, place in the community, employment, health and future."

Sue wrote, "I use Facebook for support. I am involved in two groups that help support both my sobriety and PTSD."

Janet says Facebook is great. She relocated about 7 years ago and only visits with friends back home once a year. It is practically her only contact with family members she hasn't seen in 26 years or hasn't yet met in person. She is also a part of a Certified Peer Specialist support group on Facebook.

Carol says face-to-face contact can be more soothing, but also more challenging. For her, Facebook is fast and fun, though she can get anxiety about not having time to keep up with everyone. She finds Twitter to be a complex puzzle, but that it is fun to connect worldwide. She says a crisis via electronics is scarier than face-to-face.

Caroline uses social media to stay connected. She doesn't post private struggles on open platforms like Facebook or Twitter. She uses email and texting for more private conversations around giving and receiving support.

Dana Carl uses Facebook Book to talk to one of her supports. Sometimes when she is feeling bad, she doesn't want the face-to-face contact.

Lora has used Facebook for support as well as Face Time when she was on the brink of crisis. It helped bring her back to herself. It's not as helpful to her as face-to-face. However, sometimes that's not possible, when you may need someone most, so she is thankful to have a way to still be able to get the support she needs.

Tom says that within the Veteran community, they are seeing a rise in the use of social media to get assistance. He says they have huge networks of support groups and resources that are provided from across the country. He says that most people like this type of interaction because face-to-face contact has not worked or they were not able to get appointments frequent enough to address issues in a timely way. He says that the brotherhood/sisterhood in the military makes it easier to connect through social media and provide guidance because it is with another person that has been there and done that. He feels that "the downfall to using social media is that everyone becomes an expert, what we call in the military 'barracks lawyers,' and some of the information may not be correct for an individual situation. For instance, I have seen an individual helping another person in a serious situation and the helping person gets 'triggered' by the person they are helping and the situation becomes very serious." He says, "As much as social media is a helper, it also can become an issue."

Ian says, "I use the Facebook messenger app as well as the regular Facebook site on my phone as social media. I find that both are very helpful to me in communicating with friends and family. I have even joined in some good old fashioned discussion with others about my life and living with Obsessive

Compulsive Disorder. I was a patient as well as a client of psychiatric center for many years. Now, by the grace of God and getting myself back on track, I have my own studio apartment. What's good about Facebook is that with the Facebook messenger app I can still be close to my friends and I don't have to go far. I love it."

Minnie says, "I use Facebook because it makes it easy for me to stay connected with many people across the state. The feedback from many has helped me reach a higher level of self-esteem, believe it or not."

Hiede says that there are three Facebook pages that she regularly uses for support, and she's done chat rooms a few times when her need was pressing. She doesn't usually do chat rooms and prefers face-to-face, but she also doesn't want to wake the people she loves at 2:00 a.m. She says, "Fortunately, there is always someone awake on the Internet."

Wendy says, "I use it and I feel more connected, but face-to-face is so much better."

Jode says she is on the road a lot so virtual support is essential for her. It is part of her WRAP.

Donna says, "It is weird when I think of it. I provide peer support services, but have such a hard time interacting with 'regular' people, or I guess anybody outside the mental health world. I have intense fears, like trouble going into a grocery store alone. Social media allows me to have a connection with my family. They don't visit or call. At least I can watch their posts and see how they're doing. Social media can be a lifeline and a way to practice skills. The distance keeps you safe, but still the face-to-face human connection can't be replaced. But sometimes many of us can't get that in our lives."

Grace says it's easier to use technology because she doesn't have to uphold standards of the happy majority for face-to-face interactions, such as clean clothes, an energetic demeanor, and a smiling face. It also enables her to break off with people more easily. It's less stressful because there's not so much stimulation such as noise, odors, bright lights and excessive numbers of people around. She does say that she tends to meet too many "psychiatric consumers" online and listening to them can be very triggering because they are very accepting of psychiatry—mental health believers. She tends to unfriend those people as much as possible.

Kathleen says, "I use the WRAP app on my phone often. It's succinct and I always have it with me. I belong to two Facebook groups that are helpful. I've moved twice in two years, so I don't have a lot of face-to-face interactions yet. Facebook Messenger is great for a quick check-in, or texting someone lets me know if they're available. With certain people, I'd rather have written communication because the sound of their voices (and what I perceive as disapproval) is re-activating for me. I dislike webinars because there are lots of technological glitches and I get impatient. I prefer to listen to a recorded webinar after-the-fact when it is convenient for me and the recording has been edited. My energy is high very early in the morning and I usually can't stay up to travel to a face-to-face support group in the evening and then travel back home at night."

Paul says, "I believe we only exist in relation to one another so in that sense yes, technology is very valuable."

Marcie does not use technology for Peer Support. She says, "I use my WRAP tools and I also attend my support groups every week. That keeps me grounded for the entire week and weekend. I try not to dwell on my depression."

Wendy says, "I use social media every day. It gives me the opportunity to look at things when I need to. It gives me a variety of resources. It lets me read things and think about how I can improve my life. It gives me the opportunity to look at myself and think about the things that may be impacting my life. It allows me to take a journey of self-discovery and build up my recovery and resiliency toolbox. Without social media there are times when I wouldn't have anybody I feel like I could to talk to. A lot can happen in a week while you are waiting to see a counselor. A lot of relationships can be destroyed. Social media allows for a healthy resource to access the right care at the right time."

Raven says, "I teach WRAP here and they love it. I created 'Site Keeper of the Feather.' We uplift each other. We use positive affirmations. We have Wellness Toolboxes that have so many things we help each other to use. The people in the class that I teach are some of the administrators of the site. The site was a dream to see if it would spark any interest. We have been online now about 3 months. I wasn't sure this dream was going to go, but we now have 190 members. We have collaborated with another closed group and it's awesome. They are also a support group and it's just growing and the love and the support is so wonderful to see. We all share everything—the happy, good, bad, sad, the ups the downs, because we have each other to help each other. WRAP has changed so many lives—lawyers, doctors, everyday people. WRAP YOUR WORLD IN EMPOWERMENT AND SELF-ESTEEM."

Debby says someone posted the link to "7 Cups of Tea," a worldwide, 24 hour Peer Support chat. "It's pretty good if you need to just connect with someone, just anyone at all, at 3 am."

Michael says social media (Facebook) helps him relax after stressful days and certain life situations. He says, "I can post to friends and get responses and positive feedback."

Rokus says Facebook is a powerful tool for Peer Support. "I encourage people with lived experience that join my group, Learning-experiences to The USA (more than 100 people), to connect with each other. I am proud to say that people found a way to connect and support each other through daily life and thus social media. I think we haven't seen anything yet. It can be bigger and I think we should encourage people to do it."

Karen says social media is becoming increasingly important. "Even in a crowd of people face-to-face you will find them chatting on their phones." She has used virtually all forms of social media, or can figure out how.

Jennifer uses programs such as Facebook because some of her supporters live out of town. She prefers face-to-face communication because she receives more validation and because she can tell that the supporter is paying attention. She says that when she uses social media, she doesn't know if the supporter is distracted by something else.

Cheryl uses all types of social media for support. She says, "I use Facebook, Twitter, and text to reach out. I am always happy when I am able to connect face-to-face but I am simply on the road too much. Most recently, at the passing of my husband, I felt wrapped in love and support from my virtual friends, as well as my face-to-face supporters."

Veronica says face-to-face is fantastic. However, when the session is done, having a worldwide connection to peers, family and friends, makes the difference. She says, "I used to feel alone. Not anymore. Since I joined Facebook I connected again. I can be a support to people and be supported with no money involved. It's a beautiful thing when strangers encourage, love and even grieve together. It's like a giant WRAP smile."

Patricia says, "I use Facebook a lot! I run a Facebook group called 'Walk with me thru our issues.' I'm glad there's Facebook and social media! I don't drive, so when I can't get to face-to-face it's nice to just go on Facebook for a chat with my friends and play the games on the apps. I use both social media and face-to-face."

Audrey says, "I like to use Facebook and Twitter both for support and to share knowledge and events. I am working on a Facebook page about using my own WRAP plan. I keep up to date with WRAP, Open Dialogue and Intentional Peer Support. I am a member of a few support groups and have found I can help as well as receive help. Peer Support can be so effective. Of course you have to be careful in such groups, as some people can be in a bad place, but everyone seems very mindful of what they say and often post warnings if they feel what they have to say may trigger others. There is an immediacy with this type of support. You can be supported in minutes rather than going through doctors, the emergency room, or anything like that. The immediacy has, for me, defused a crisis before it became one, as I posted what I was feeling much earlier in the process than I would have consulted a 'professional'."

Joanne says, "I am a Certified Peer Support Specialist. But even before I became a CPS, I always liked doing things face-to-face, or with a note or letter (post). And last with a telephone call. I am from 'the old school' and was brought up to send thank you notes for gifts, and such. The letter is becoming obsolete. I do use the internet, but my first response is to use face-to-face."

Trusty says, "I use both. My face-to-face support is a Recovery Group, provided by my County's Community Mental Health, led by a paid Peer Support Coordinator and then I have a support friend from church who is a retired College Professor who taught Mental Health Nursing at a Nursing College. Google+ online support groups are a daily place to find mental health support but I find online communication to be very disheartening. My posts often are not even acknowledged by a 'plus,' and seldom by comments, so it's easy to feel rejection, and I have had people 'block' me, who once called me friend, without an explanation. I don't know what I said that caused them to change their mind about me. Face-to-face interaction is so much better, though not as often. Face-to-face support is safer and more trustworthy, and offers mutuality. If someone has a complaint toward me, we can address the issues together and find mutual resolution. Online communication is like a Las Vegas one-arm bandit…sometimes there's a jackpot of response from others, but mostly no…and that only exponentially adds to my mental health suffering. But like any gambling addiction, high hopes for the jackpot of affirmation drives me to spend more time than I ought to...for such a low rate of return and worse, utter rejection for which I have no recourse to fix. At least face-to-face, a resolve is almost sure to transpire...and that is where personal growth can surely occur. The goal of recovery is to improve mental and behavioral health. Online communication can foster 'road rage'...where irritations can develop and with an easy stroke of a button, anger can be muted/deleted/blocked, like an angry gesture waved at a fellow driver...blocked communication accomplishes nothing good. Although online interaction offers 24/7 support, the quality of human interaction is too unreliable for me, personally...too Dr. Jekyll/Mr. Hyde-like. On Facebook...I'm liked, not liked...that takes its toll on my self-esteem, which is vital for recovery. Face-to-face interaction builds sturdy self-esteem."

Helen says, "I have been using Facebook with increasing frequency. First and foremost, for me it is similar to communication by text or via email. I have been told by others, and I have experienced in my own past, that electronic communication (by any means) was a true first-step in breaking isolation in a non-threatening way. We are now in an era where many have grown up with electronic communication. For me, it does not equal "face-to-face" encounters. Yet Facebook has allowed me to reach out to a larger number of people than I could have with in-person conversations.

"The evolution of this technology and inclusion of 'emoticons' allows me to pass along feelings, which I previously assumed the reader would 'know' by reading my words. I have found that in my emails of old, much was lost in the two-dimensional words. That said, I have found that Facebook has served to enhance my connections with others.

"A few examples: I have reached out to colleagues from my first Advanced WRAP Facilitators training, who have since changed employment and thus have new contact information, via Facebook messaging, and obtained their current addresses and phone numbers.

"I also feel a daily 'connection' with people who do not or no longer live in my area who are connected to WRAP and Recovery. The same holds true with Advocacy groups I am signed up with, such as 'Stop the Murphy Bill.' The latter has provided me with information and ways to contact Congress Members in 'real time' to advise them of Behavioral Health and Wellness or my position on matters we deem critical to enhance human dignity and civil rights.

"I have also been able to reconnect with people from my past. Some of these people go back to elementary school, although most are related to music and high school. When visiting, I have now been able to meet with many of these people. Several of them will be attending my upcoming wedding, which brings great joy and continuity to my life."

Joe says, "I use Facebook and SMART recovery online meetings and tools, but I also go to AA and support groups for face-to-face. I find I need all of these combined to keep my recovery on track."

Carolyn says, "I belong to a support group that is fabulous. I've learned a lot about taking hold of my own recovery and Facebook has helped me out a lot."

Joyce says that technology is no comparison to face-to-face, but a good substitute at times. "The feedback is not from a professional and most are talking about being strong and motivational. Professionals are about moving people forward in positive and constructive ways."

Tiffany says, "I've tried to use technology, but it doesn't seem to be as effective as seeing someone face-to-face, or hearing their voice over the phone. In a pinch, it works, though."

Barb says, "Now that I no longer work in the mental health field, getting on Facebook has helped greatly when I need to touch base with supports that live far and wide. It is not as good as face-to-face. However, it is much better than not being able to get in contact at all."

Kathyann says "I use Facebook for support, but I do it through closed groups because I do not feel comfortable having everything open. The small groups I use include one for my health, one for creativity and one as a forum to talk about how we are building WRAP in the area where I live. I enjoy long phone calls with friends, writing letters and cards to friends and I am part of a Franciscan Fellowship where we grow together in music and spirituality."

Steve says, "I do private message in Facebook. It has actually helped me through a Crisis."

Julie says she uses Facebook and it works, especially when she is communicating about fighting stigma against mental illness.

Maureen says "I have used Facebook in closed groups. It's a way to connect at any hour of the day or night. But, for me at least, it is not as effective as face-to-face. I prefer the more personal touch of being there with others, seeing them and being able to get a hug if I need it. I also have access to a warm line but am not always able to get through to it right away."

Susan says, "I have used WRAP in my own wellness, but due to life issues have recently relocated several times. Facebook has allowed me to stay connected to people who have been members of my support team from wherever I happen to be. I share inspirational stories and affirmations, as well as opinions on various issues that affect our lives. I find information that the mainstream media either can't or won't report on. News that might be censored otherwise can go viral over social media. It allows communication around the globe, so alternative perspectives can be gathered. Hope is a universal language. We can learn a lot from seeking alternative perspectives, as long as we are open to change, and those we communicate with are respectful of our emotional state. The only downfall I see with social media is that you can't tell what the person is thinking. You can't see facial expressions and body language, so the person could be only halfway listening or thinking of their response instead of truly trying to understand.

"I use social media, and I find it helpful when I am isolated from my support network. I do, however, like face-to-face support. When I am able, I connect in person. When no one is available, I will connect with someone who will listen. As long as there is life, there is hope. Never give up hope. I will find someone to affirm my hope, even if it's 2 a.m."

Rosa says, "I utilize an app on my phone. It's connected to a website but you can access the forum through an app. There are many categories for support groups. It's great because it's easy to use. I really like it because I feel like I can connect with people that I otherwise would not connect with in person. For example, in my support group there are doctors, nurses, teachers, CEOs. It's really amazing how this support group can bring a diverse group of people together. I have never been in a support group with someone who is in a higher position. It's nice that the app brings us together and we are able to see that all people of any socio-economic class need support and we are able to provide that for one another. One thing I also like about this particular support group is that you are able to maintain your anonymity so that titles and labels don't matter. You are simply there to discuss and support."

Jen says, "Nothing works for me more than the soft voice and touch of a friend and peer who understands."

Martin says, "I am primary support and caregiver to my best friend who lives with mental health issues, chronic fatigue syndrome (CFS/ME) and fibromyalgia. We met on Facebook four years ago and have grown close, having a mutually caring and supportive friendship completely online. I live in the United Kingdom, she is 3000 miles away in the US. We use a wide range of technologies (primarily Facebook, Skype and Twitter) to keep in touch and to share our worlds, both with each other and with other like-minded and like-hearted people all over the world. We are proud to have recently joined the Skype Ambassador program as Ambassadors for Social Good. We are passionate about sharing what we have learned and are writing a book based on our experiences as friends. Our vision is a world where no one is too far away to be cared for, or to care."

Richard says, "I've heard that some people with Obsessive Compulsive Disorder, who can't tolerate being physically in Peer Support groups, use online chat support groups that are very helpful. I know people with social anxiety who can't attend support groups in person, or get much from a classroom experience, but do well with online support groups and online courses. I personally don't use social media for support, but I do keep up with friends via emails and Facebook, which is a kind of support."

Lindy writes, "We now live in a world that has no start or stop to it. The freedom is at our fingertips to build relationships in different ways."

Sandra says, "I never stop being grateful that we are blessed with all these technological gadgets, like computers, iPhones, Kindle and the various programs and Apps. I really do not know how I would cope without these and losing them would be a very, very big Trigger for me!

"Facebook is very important to me! I more or less journal on there and many people say that they have learned a lot from me about what it is like to be 'bipolar.' I get lots of encouragement and support from Facebook friends, whether they are ex-pupils (often), also bipolar friends that I met in the 1990s online, church friends, or, sometimes, people who, first of all, only played online Scrabble with me, but have come to 'know' me, follow me and support me. There are several groups, especially, where I find personal support: 'Bipolars Supporting Bipolars' and a private one we have where I live, connected to my church and others, called 'Encouraging Women,' where we can ask for, and get prayers. However, I must say that I have found that I can't really use that if I'm in a crisis, they just don't understand, well, some of them! I have friends who encourage me on Facebook all the time and it goes both ways! Facebook is also a way to keep in touch with other WRAP Coordinators, everywhere. Of course there are the WRAP groups, WRAP Facilitators groups, closed groups and a Mental Health Recovery Group as well."

Courses for everyone, from beginners at WRAP and Peer Support, to Advanced Level Facilitators.

Improve skills, enhance personal relationships, increase hope and quality of life.

Contact Us!

Copeland Center
FOR WELLNESS AND RECOVERY

P.O. Box 6471
Brattleboro, VT 05302
802-254-5335
WWW.COPELANDCENTER.COM
INFO@COPELANDCENTER.COM